UNSOCIAL MEDIA MANAGEMENT FOR BUSINESS

THE 'HOW-TO' GUIDE FOR MANAGING ONLINE DRAMA TO BOOST YOUR BOTTOM LINE

By
Brandy Booth

FREE BONUS

Thank you for buying my book.
As an added bonus, I've included a free copy of
Charged Up Marketing. In it, you'll discover a
simple technique to literally energize your audience
about your business or brand.
Download yours now to energize your bottom line!

http://www.unsocialmediamanagement.com/bonus

UNSOCIAL MEDIA MANAGEMENT FOR BUSINESS

www.unsocialmediamanagement.com

Copyright 2017 © Catalyst Publishing

First Edition 2017

Table of Contents

Foreword

You don't have to look far to find social media experts these days. You'll find them at every turn, telling you how to conquer the business world online with Facebook, Twitter, and other platforms. There's no shortage of business books either, and they all come at it from the positive, glowing side of how to harness the amazing power of social media for massive growth. They're all focused on social media marketing.

The only problem? They're leaving out one important aspect of social media: how to manage the conversations already going on, especially negative ones. No one is talking about it, until now. Brandy Booth wrote *Unsocial Media Management* to show you how to manage negative social media situations, turn them around, and profit from them.

This book should be within arm's reach of every business owner, CEO, social media manager, entrepreneur, and public relations professional. If you have to deal with people online, this book is for you. And Brandy is the perfect guy to deliver the message. He isn't just giving advice that sounds good. This is time-tested, in-the-trenches, proven advice gained from a couple decades of real-life experience.

Brandy is a successful copywriter who helps businesses craft messages that get customers to act. He also works for a major corporation and spent almost ten years resolving conflicts between employees, managers, engineers, contractors, and suppliers. He knows how to deal with people at every level, and he'll help you manage social media situations with one end goal: to boost your bottom line.

If Dale Carnegie was alive today, this is the book he would have written. *Unsocial Media Management* is the *How to Win Friends & Influence People* for our time. You can't compare it to any others because no one has written a book like this. It's a field manual for getting along with people online and off, and Brandy is your guide.

- Steve Roller
Founder and Publisher of CafeWriter.com

Introduction

Let's be honest. Many business owners and managers feel as if social media is a gamble at best.

Sure, it might be useful for connecting with customers or communicating with your workforce, but there's always a chance that something could go terribly wrong.

There are too many negative people out there to think things will always go right. And it only takes one negative experience, right?

We've all heard horror stories about bad social media ruining a company's image. Nobody wants to deal with that fallout.

And it isn't a very positive place for personal users either, with the political drama, arguing, and negativity we seem to see (on social media) in general.

No, social media doesn't appear to be a wise investment for today's businesses at all.

Besides, if you think about it, most businesses specialize in whatever business they're in, not social media management. Why invest in something you know so little about that has so much negativity surrounding it?

IT'S VERY SIMPLE.

Social media is where your clients, customers, employees, and fans are at.

Period.

It's where they spend their free time. It's where they focus their attention. They understand how to use it, and it's familiar to them.

Social media provides a way for people to reach out to the world when the chains of their life have them shackled to a job or some other monotonous task that requires their physical presence but not their full attention.

A lot of users are addicted to social media. It's a getaway. Whenever they get a break, their thumb mindlessly taps the icon, and they instantly go into a newsfeed-induced trance.

In fact, a good percentage of your target audience is scrolling this very second. It's what they're doing, and they're not going to stop doing it any time soon.

They know a lot of what they see is negative. They don't care. Most complain about it, scroll down, and complain about it some more. They just keep scrolling.

They might quit for a day or a month, but they always go back.

If you were to ask them, most would agree that negativity (in various forms) is the biggest problem on social media.

I feel the same way.

But the way I see it, if negativity is the biggest problem on social media, that also makes it the biggest *opportunity*.

You Can Manage Unsocial Media

Like any other problem in life, negativity on social media is just another challenge to overcome.

In *Unsocial Media Management for Business*, you'll learn to handle any negative situation with ease.

It doesn't matter if you're:

- A **Customer Service Representative** dealing with angry feedback from an irate customer or jealous competitor.
- A **Corporate Manager** trying to drive tough cultural change down through the ranks of your company.
- A **Blogger** trying to learn to become a more powerful influencer as "trolls" call you a liar.
- An **Entrepreneur** launching an information product while a group of naysayers heckles and harasses you.

- The **President** of a nonprofit seeking to influence and educate others on a controversial purpose or cause.

All the knowledge you need to overcome these challenges (and more) is inside this book.

Releasing the Brakes

Negativity is like a big anchor tied directly to your bottom line.

It doesn't matter where it is, if you have a negativity problem anywhere in your business (value) stream, it's holding you back from success.

Unhappy customers. Disgruntled employees. Dissatisfied clients. A look in the mirror...

You know where it's at.

Negativity anywhere in your business is costing you money.

How much money? It all depends, but it's probably a lot.

Let me put it this way. When I said that negativity is the biggest business opportunity on social media, I wasn't kidding.

In fact, I believe that *Unsocial Media Management* is BY FAR the biggest economic opportunity on the whole internet.

Of course I do. I wrote this book, right?

But there are a lot of reasons why I believe this.

The biggest one is that freeing your business from negativity and drama allows the things you already do to work better.

Your marketing efforts will pay off better. Your ads will get better click-throughs. Your products will garner better reviews.

But your bottom line isn't just connected to an increase in sales. It's also tied to your workforce. Your production employees. Your managers. Your customer service representatives.

Removing negativity from your workforce and supply chain could make the difference between employees who require discipline for not doing their jobs versus ones who make good decisions for the business, whether you're watching them or not.

But there's another important reason to focus on continuously improving your workforce communications.

In today's changing economy, it's critical for companies to be able to adapt to change if they're going to stay viable. Believe me, change is a lot easier to manage when you're not fighting against silly rumors, lies, and drama.

Like I said, there's big opportunity in negativity.

Who Am I?

I wrote this book because I understand the problem of businesses being held back by negativity on social media, both customer-based and workforce-based.

I also understand the solution.

Until eight years ago, I was a committeeman and contract negotiator in a large trade union.

I bargained wages, benefits, and working conditions for over 3,000 members and represented them on the factory floor whenever contractual issues arose.

I spent almost 10 years resolving conflicts between employees, managers, engineers, contractors, safety, and suppliers. I wrote competitive bids for skilled trades work, proposals for new customer contracts, and last-chance agreements for employees about to lose their jobs.

It was also my job to explain to the membership why our bargaining team took concessions during tough economic times, so I built a Facebook group to keep them informed of pending changes.

A group of radicals IMMEDIATELY tore me apart.

Facebook was new back then, and all the top union leaders tried to discourage me from interacting with members on social media during negotiations for liability reasons. But I didn't stop.

I knew that to get those agreements ratified and for our site to have a viable future, the members needed to understand and support the contractual changes.

Through trial and error, I learned how to respectfully communicate the details to the members while "trolls" constantly argued with me, called me a liar, and smeared my name on every post or comment. (They also wrote about me in bathroom stalls throughout the complex!)

I'll admit, I lost my cool a few times, but I eventually found ways to keep things civil and productive despite these self-proclaimed "Factory Rats" constantly trying to derail my every conversation.

Some of the things they said still leave me shaking my head today. Some of it was creative. All of it was offensive.

I couldn't blame them for being angry though. Those were tough agreements to negotiate with Management, and even tougher to "sell" to the membership.

If you're wondering how tough a collective bargaining agreement can be, consider this: During my time in office, our complex was spun off from the parent company, bankrupted twice, nearly closed, and ultimately sold to the Chinese Government.

Those were tough contracts to negotiate and ratify!

But then things got worse for me.

First, my marriage fell apart, and I went through a nasty divorce.

Then my best friend and Bargaining Chairman died of a heart attack from the stress of these negotiations.

Life was chaos. I couldn't find peace and quiet anywhere. Not at home. Not at work. Not even on the ride between the two. Not anywhere.

To help with the noise in my head, I began listening to spiritual teachers like Wayne Dyer, Eckhart Tolle, Ram Dass, Abraham Hicks, Thich Nhat Hanh, and others.

I learned about stress and negativity and that we can control our point of focus to create better outcomes. I learned that some of the best opportunities come along during periods of tough change.

And that's exactly what happened...

To help the workforce transition through the crazy changes, Management had hired a consulting firm that specialized in training people to focus on the opportunity that presents itself during tough periods of change.

This point resonated with me because I'd just learned it from the spiritual gurus I'd been listening to.

So I became a facilitator of their material and saw how people could create their own reality by changing the way they think. I learned how we put roadblocks in our own way and that we can't easily recognize an opportunity if we don't expect it.

When Management offered a buyout during an economic downturn, several people from my sessions quit their jobs to chase their dreams. I'm still friends with many of them today, and some of their success stories are quite remarkable.

As I started to turn my attention to more positive situations, I lost my drive for interacting with the union members and managers who never seemed to want to get along.

But I needed something more to do than simply working on the factory floor as a millwright-welder. I'd learned a lot through those years, and I wanted to put my knowledge to work.

Because of my experience in writing contracts and proposals, a friend suggested I check out online copywriting, or writing promotions for products and services that market their offerings online. I studied hard and learned to craft compelling promotions designed to attract customers and convert sales.

I also took a special interest in social media marketing and learned everything I could about how businesses use it to create a personalized connection with their target audience.

But as I began helping to manage business accounts, I noticed the same problem with nearly every one of them.

Business owners did great until someone negative or harassing showed up. Then they became frustrated, overwhelmed, and eventually lost interest.

It didn't matter what kind of drama it was, it killed their momentum.

Communication was being sabotaged by radicals. Jealous competitors were leaving damaging reviews. Business owners were reeling with confusion and frustration.

And then it dawned on me that this problem wasn't much different from the negativity in the union forums I used to manage.

In fact, a lot of their tactics were nearly the same. Although I'd dreaded dealing with negative people back in my negotiating days, I now recognized this problem as an opportunity. And with so much negativity all over social media, it was a big one.

That's why I wrote *Unsocial Media Management*. This is where life has brought me. It has all led up to this.

Businesses need to learn to understand, prepare for, engage with, and eliminate negativity on social media. They need to know how to deal with it whether it shows up in their customer base or in their own workforce.

Dealing with extremely negative people on a regular basis allowed me to play around with different communication techniques and make adjustments as necessary.

It wasn't pleasant, easy, or neat, and believe me - there was **plenty** of trial and error.

Some of the tactics I studied in marketing helped me to conceptualize the techniques in this book. I incorporated lessons I had learned from spiritual teachers into them as well.

I packaged it all up as neatly as I could, and I can't wait to share it with you.

But before we go any further, I want to tell you one more thing about me.

I have a genuine passion for watching people overcome obstacles and break barriers. I love helping today's businesses recognize the opportunity that almost always comes with tough change.

Once you free yourself from negativity, the sky's the limit. And that's really what this book is all about.

You see, the negativity that plagues social media isn't the primary focus of *Unsocial Media Management for Business*.

The real focus is how to leverage the true potential of social media to grow your business once the drama and negativity have been effectively dealt with.

Unsocial Media Management for Business – The Overview

To overcome any challenge in life, you must first understand it.

In Chapter One of *Unsocial Media Management for Business*, you'll come to understand negative people in a way that makes them easy to manage.

You'll learn who they are, what they do, and the overall effect they have on social media.

You'll also be made aware of the ONE GOAL that all negative people try to achieve when they harass you, so you'll never fall into their traps again.

Chapter Two prepares you to engage them in a way that's consistent with your main purpose for being online.

Like any other conflict, unsocial media is much easier to manage if you take the time to prepare beforehand.

You'll define what a "win" looks like, learn how companies communicate from a "platform" by branding themselves, and see what it takes to become a powerful social media influencer.

The saying "You get back what you put out" is 100% true on social media. To have better social media, you must put out better social media - even when you're being harassed.

By the end of Chapter Two, you'll know how to do it.

In Chapter Three, you'll master the art of responding to harassment, negativity, and insults in an **authentic** manner.

Being authentic is the most effective way to become a trusted social media influencer, which is the basis for powerful online marketing.

Although the person harassing you probably isn't your target audience, that doesn't mean your target audience isn't listening.

On the contrary. The first thing I learned in copywriting school was that there's no better marketing "hook" than live drama. They're ALL paying attention.

By the end of Chapter Three, you'll know how to respond to harassment in a way that gives your target audience something authentic to think about.

Chapter Four is titled "If the Gloves Must Come Off" for good reason.

It's dedicated to that one special person who just won't leave you alone. There comes a time when you have to put an end to the nonsense so you can get back down to business.

In this chapter, you'll learn to take out the trash in a classy, genuine sort of way. (I struggled with this for years and only recently figured out an effective solution that didn't involve blocking, reporting, or unfriending the offender.)

Chapter Five is called "Social Media and the Future of Your Business," and it's exactly what you'd expect from a chapter with that name. If you're still trying to decide whether or not there is a future for social media in your business, you don't want to miss this chapter.

In Chapter 6: "Ideas that Work," you'll see how small businesses, large corporations, and powerful influencers are exploding their businesses by leveraging social media's unique strengths in a variety of cutting-edge ways.

In Chapter 7: "Energize Your Bottom Line," I'll teach you to leverage the **true power** of social media after all the drama and negativity has been effectively dealt with.

You'll learn a powerful new process to *literally* charge your audience up about your product, service, or brand.

Your business will never be the same after you've learned the lessons in this book, and neither will you.

Powerful Communication

Social media's unique strengths make it an extremely powerful communication tool.

Never before could you become "friends" with someone in one click, have instant access to what they like and dislike, and discuss any topic you choose in a group or private setting from the palm of your hand, wherever you're at.

That's HUGE – and it's just the tip of the iceberg.

There are a lot of other opportunities to leverage social media's unique strengths to grow in any way you choose.

But they're only available after you've given unsocial media the boot.

Confident Social Media

This part of the introduction is where I make you a promise of the benefits you'll experience from reading my book.

While there's no way to guarantee you'll become the next internet millionaire or the most powerful social media influencer of all time, I **can** promise you this:

If you apply the knowledge and lessons in this book to your own situation, I promise you a confident social media experience.

There's a lot to be said for being confident in any given situation. Confident social media means you won't have to worry about anyone bullying you, making you mad, or trying to ruin your business by blowing up your "wall."

Confident social media means the conflict you used to worry about will be easy for you to leverage into better things. Confident social media means social media without stress, drama, and negativity.

Enough is Enough

Regardless of whether your business has (or plans to have) a social media presence or not, people are still going to talk about you on the internet.

There are a multitude of ways for attackers to create posts and leave comments about your business online. There are blogs, review sites, social media groups, articles, white papers, and countless other places they can go to leave feedback about you and your company.

It's best to learn how to deal with unsocial media rather than ignore it or pretend it doesn't exist.

So how about it? Are you ready to learn how to manage the negativity on social media, so you're able to protect your business and move forward, despite the best efforts of the people harassing you?

Are you ready for Unsocial Media Management?

Turn the page, and let's get started.

CHAPTER I

Understanding Negative People

Most of us try to ignore them. Some of us confront them. But if we want to put an end to negative people constantly harassing us or our businesses online, what we really need to do is UNDERSTAND them.

I'm not talking about becoming their guidance counselor or psychologist. I'm talking about the type of understanding we aim for whenever we encounter a tough challenge.

Think of it like trying to find footholds on a rock face you're trying to climb. Once you gain traction, the challenge becomes a lot easier. So, let's take a deeper look into why negative people do what they do, so we can learn to overcome the challenges they present to you and your business.

Who are they?

We think of them as "trolls" that hide behind dimly-lit computer screens in the darkest of basements. They lunge from the cyber-shadows to attack innocent people and companies who only want to market their products and services or share a message with the world.

They have no conscience or morals. They're rude, disrespectful, and outright mean.

"Troll" is the perfect label for these reclusive, hideous beasts whose only function is being a menace to society.

Other than that, they're completely useless.

Although this is how we sometimes perceive them, it's not how they really are. In reality, they're standing right next to us. They're our coworkers and the people who sell us groceries. They're the cable guy, the banker, or the quiet kid at the mall.

Sometimes, they're even the people who watch our own children while we're at work. The fact of the matter is that these negative people are just like us in a lot of ways.

They get out of bed and put their pants on every morning just like you and I do. And regardless of which subject or situation triggered their emotion and caused them to attack you, it's important to remember that they're not all rotten to the core.

Why are they so negative?

In business, people can get mad and lash out at you for a variety of reasons.

They could have had a bad experience with your product or service. They could be a jealous competitor looking to steal some of your business away by smearing your name.

If it's an employee that's causing problems, maybe they're still upset about the across-the-board pay cut that happened two years ago.

There are an endless number of reasons why people could get mad at you or your business. If you have a specific negative person in mind, you may have a pretty good idea of what their problem or issue is with you.

But overall, I find it helpful to try to understand a person's degree of negativity by classifying them into one of three groups. Knowing which group they're in will help you to understand the most effective way to interact with them when the time comes to respond.

#1: The "Bad Day" Group
The first group of people are those who are just having a bad day. Bad days can bring out the worst in people.

They stub their toe when they get out of bed, spill coffee on their favorite shirt, and get a flat tire on their way to work.

In this state of mind, everything appears negative to them.

They might misunderstand the intent of your post on social media when they see it and choose to lash out at you for no apparent reason. They might feel that your product or service is inferior to someone else's and go completely overboard in letting you know.

(You might have discovered their negative comment in the middle of your OWN bad day and be tempted to act out of character. Don't do it! We'll cover why in Chapter Two.)

Regardless of the reason, these are people who generally aren't negative or outspoken.

Of the three groups, they're the most likely to come back in a day or two and apologize.

#2: The "Stuck in a Rut" Group
The second group of people are those who are caught in a bigger rut than those who are just having a bad day.

They may be struggling financially or dealing with health or family issues. They could have experienced some sort of trauma that caused them to take a hard stance on the issue you're butting heads over.

Whatever the reason, they're acting out because something has them frustrated. They may be irate that something changed, or that something won't change in the way they believe it should.

They may be angry about the product or service you provide, or they may feel like your business, idea, or stance on a subject is all wrong. They're not negative overall, but they're definitely not in a good place when certain topics come up.

People who argue about "the hot button issues" (politics, religion, celebrities, or whatever drama mass media is selling) normally fall into this group.

They sometimes contribute good information in other areas of life on social media, but you may never know it if you only encounter them when they access your business page to complain about your terrible customer service.

Their actions are a little more predictable than the "bad day" group, but they're used to defending their issue and unlikely to budge on their opinion – even when faced with undeniable facts.

#3: The "Negative Nancy" Group
This is the group that can't seem to say anything nice at all.

They focus exclusively on why an idea or suggestion *won't* work, bring up the worst-case scenario in any given situation, and never offer a viable solution to the problem at hand.

They chronically complain about everything, look for reasons to start fights, and are never happy with the resolution to any issue.

They're a customer service nightmare.

They love the fact that you can't just ignore them and walk away on social media like you can in real life.

If you tell them the glass is half full, they say it's half empty and that there's a crack in it.

If they were given a million dollars, they'd be mad that someone else got a million and one. If they hear something changed for the better, they say it won't last.

Many Negative Nancies use false screen names and profile pictures so they can harass others without having to pay any price for their actions.

They tend to run in groups because they don't get along well with regular people, and they attack like sharks if they think there's weakness in your logic, point, or cause.

These people are just plain unhappy.

Sometimes I feel bad for the people in the Negative Nancy group.

I've gone through tough times, too. There were plenty of days where I felt like the whole world was against me. For a little while, I was even the bad guy who went overboard and lashed out at others who didn't deserve it.

But I was always able to find my way out of the funk and refocus on good things.

The Negative Nancy group just doesn't seem to be able to feel better. To me, that's sad.

Regardless of how you feel about negative people, it's important to try to understand which group they fit into.

This information will come in handy when the time comes to respond if that's what you decide to do....

What do they do?

Negative people have only ONE goal in mind when they attack you or your business on social media.

They want to gain control over your energy and focus. Some of them are really good at it, judging from my past experiences in certain groups and forums.

You might not want to admit that you've allowed these bullies to control you, but if you've engaged in their nonsense at all, you've allowed them to control you in some way.

To understand why it works so well for them (and how to make sure it NEVER happens again), grab a partner and check out the "Hand-Push" lesson.

The "Hand-Push" Lesson

Tell the person facing you to raise their hand like they're being sworn in at court.

Put your hand up to mirror theirs and then begin to push.

Without being told to do so, they WILL push back.

Even though you controlled where they put their hand in the first place, they'll still resist your push if you don't explain what you're doing.

This is basic human nature. We try to hold our position and fight to do so without realizing we're even doing it. It's the main reason why people are so resistant to change.

It's also the reason why negative people can get to you on social media. They know it's in your nature to push back.

They bait you with negative comments and insulting remarks, trying to entice you into engaging with them so they can redirect your energy away from your cause or opinion. If you even start to push back, you lose.

This is a critical point to remember so you don't fall into the traps they set by responding while in an emotional state.

You'll learn a much better way to respond to their nonsense in Chapter 3.

Where do they do it?

Negative people strike anywhere they can leave a comment online.

They harass businesses on blog posts, articles, product reviews, in groups, and anywhere else that draws their attention at any given moment.

These people have no boundaries or rules.

I've seen them viciously attack others in forums on being better parents, blogs that help families cope with a loved one who has brain cancer, and even in the comments on articles about how to be happier.

They don't care about your business or what others think about their comments. The only thing that's important is that they're right and you're wrong, no matter what you're talking about or where you're at.

There really isn't any place that's safe from their spite.

Why do they do it?

There are a lot of reasons why certain people decide to make negative comments or harass others. Sometimes their motives are easy to understand, and sometimes they're a complete mystery.

Maybe they had a bad experience with your product or service. Maybe they aren't happy with their life and have just gotten used to being negative. They may disagree with your opinion or a cause you stand for. They might not like you as a person. Or maybe, they're just being a bully because they can.

Some of them do a good job of convincing others that their cause is worthy (and yours isn't) or their opinion is valid (and yours isn't).

I've actually found myself on the same side of a contract vote with some really negative people, but in complete disagreement with the ideas and tactics they were using to fight with.

I wanted specific changes. They wanted anarchy.

Our vote was still a "NO!" but for completely different reasons.

To be effective in dealing with any negative person, it helps to know why they're negative. Usually, they're up front about it, unless you're dealing with a jealous competitor who is trying to sabotage you.

Regardless of why they're doing it, take comfort in the fact that you'll soon be able to leverage their negative feedback to create a positive outcome.

How do they affect us?

Many business owners won't even create a social media presence because they're certain things will go bad. It's no secret that unsocial media can damage a company's bottom line if it gets too far out of hand. This has been a problem for businesses since social media first became a marketing tool.

It's easy to understand how scandal and drama can damage a company's reputation. We've all seen those high-profile examples of business owners and employees who made terrible choices on social media or on camera.

Hopefully, you won't have to deal with anything like that.

Most normal business owners just run into regular customer service issues and "trolls" who want to start trouble. They'll leave bad reviews, argue about the quality and value of your product, and clog up your marketing efforts with insults.

They might not ruin your business, but they definitely cost you money in the long run. They'll steal your momentum and make you wonder if social media is worth the trouble.

Negative people who work for you have the same effect on your bottom line as bad reviews. They cost you money. Left unmanaged, problems of this nature can spread through your company just like any other online virus.

The bottom line is that negative people have a negative effect on your bottom line.

Until now.

Negative People and You

We've spent all of Chapter One so far learning how to understand negative people. But... the BIGGEST thing you need to understand about negative people isn't really about negative people at all.

It's about YOU.

More specifically, it's about the way you FEEL when you encounter their harassment and insults.

Have you ever met someone who knew exactly what to say to instantly make you furious?

The comments that make you the angriest or cause you to feel the worst are called your "emotional triggers." It's extremely important to understand what your emotional triggers are. If the person harassing you knows them better than you do, they could cause you to lash out in an unprofessional way.

We all have those "special" friends and relatives who make poor social media choices.

When we think about them, it's easy to understand how their actions cause their own 'unsocial media.'

They get back what they put out. You do, too. We all do.

Smart *unsocial media management* begins with you. That means if you want to have better social media, you have to put out better social media.

That's what we're going to discuss in Chapter Two. Turn the page to learn more.

CHAPTER 2

Preparing to Engage

"BY FAILING TO PREPARE, YOU ARE PREPARING TO FAIL."
- BENJAMIN FRANKLIN

Make no mistake about it. Unsocial media is conflict.

Like every other type of conflict, it's best if you're prepared for it when it happens.

It doesn't matter if you're talking about war, a boxing match, a chess game, an election, or any other type of competitive or conflicting situation.

If you expect to win, you must be prepared. That's why I wrote this chapter.

The first half is about preparing to put out better social media by knowing who you serve and what your business goals are.

The second half is focused on how to prepare to respond after you or your business has been attacked.

That's right. You still have time to prepare *after* you've been attacked.

That's one nice thing about being harassed on social media versus being harassed in person.

On social media, you don't have to answer back right away. You've got time to think the situation over and cool your emotions down before you act.

Most of the time you can wait 24-36 hours after an attack to do some behind-the-scenes work without saying anything. Not seeing a post for a day or so is understandable in today's busy world.

But don't ignore it and don't procrastinate. Deal with it.

Leaving a negative post unanswered for too long gives an attacker a sense of power by making it appear like you are purposely avoiding them. They'll point out that you've used your social media account to post and comment in other places, even if you haven't.

No matter how offended you are, remember to keep your cool. Just like in a real fight, everyone is on high alert and watching closely when that first punch is thrown. What you do next will set the stage for all the interaction to come.

A "Canned" Response

Customer Service Representatives sometimes use a "canned response" to buy more time while they investigate a complaint.

A canned response is a previously prepared statement that says something like:

"Our customers are very important to us. We're deeply sorry that you're having a negative experience.

We greatly appreciate your feedback and use it to make our business better every day.

Please allow us 24 hours to investigate the details of this issue so we can exceed your expectations in resolving the matter at hand."

Acting courteous and professional in the face of an attack puts you in control of the situation by creating the expectation of better communication.

A good canned response acknowledges that you understand there's an issue and are willing to investigate and remedy the situation if needed.

It also implements a "cooling off" period, which is a good idea whenever tempers flare.

The bottom line is that if you care about your business, your fingers will never touch the keyboard while you're upset.

Define What a "Win" Looks Like

One of the first things to do when considering how to respond to negativity on social media is to define what a win looks like.

If you're in a stock car race, you know what a win looks like.

When you win, you drive into the winner's circle and have your picture taken while holding a checkered flag and a big trophy. That sort of win is very easy to imagine.

A win is a little harder to visualize when you've just finished reading a negative review, insulting comment, or outright social media attack that's directed at you or your business.

In this situation, it's important to remember that the goal for both social and unsocial media management is exactly the same. Serve the bottom line.

That's what a win looks like. When dealing with online negativity, a win serves your bottom line and stays true to your brand.

True to Your Brand

Have you ever wondered why it feels so terrible to respond to negative comments and harassing remarks?

By being forced to respond to an attacker's bad behavior, you're deviating from your core business values.

In marketing, they'd say you're "not being true to your brand."

No kidding, right? You didn't ask to be bullied. It's not part of your "brand" to participate in drama.

And what exactly is a brand anyhow?

A **brand** is defined as a set of marketing and communication methods that help to distinguish a business from competitors and create a lasting impression in the minds of customers. [Source: Wikipedia]

In other words, your business brand is your unique way of presenting yourself and communicating with your audience.

Built properly, your brand positions you as an expert in your field and gives you a "platform" from which to communicate.

Branding also keeps customer relations on track by creating an expectation of how employees should conduct themselves when interacting with the public. It also creates a subliminal expectation of how customers should communicate with your business.

When you've purposely built a strong brand for your business, it's almost impossible for negative people to cause you to act out of character. You simply won't fall for their tricks because it wouldn't feel right.

Today's social media makes it simple to create a profile that accurately portrays your unique business brand.

In a nutshell, your brand is who you are, what you do, and why you do it.

Let's check out what it takes to build a brand that keeps you grounded and focused when an attacker tries to steal your energy.

Who are you on Social Media?

Who are you while representing your business online?

The reason I ask it this way is because we communicate differently on social media than we do in person.

Your online business self is a combination of:

- Your core business beliefs...
- The style in which you communicate...
- What you're currently focused on...
- The ideas, information, and experiences you've had...
- Your opinion or expertise on specific matters...

- The business image you portray with words and pictures...
- How others perceive your business...
- The way you handle certain situations...
- And a vast array of other factors that make your business unique.

Chances are good that your profile already does a decent job of telling people what your business does and who you serve. But it's a good idea to update your information from time to time because your business changes as you add new staff, create new products, and implement new policies.

What do You do on Social Media?

This question is an easy one for entrepreneurs, influencers, bloggers, and most small business owners. Most of you know what you do and why you do it. You use social media to promote your business, products, and services and to connect with your customers.

I'm sure that some of you think this sounds trivial, but it's extremely important to stay grounded in your core business values when you're being harassed or attacked.

If you can remain focused on the reason your business is on social media when you're thinking about making a statement that may take you in the wrong direction, you're more likely to catch yourself before making a costly mistake.

The Mission Statement

Companies use mission statements to tell the world (and to remind themselves) what they do and where they do it.

A mission statement is a short and simple (normally one sentence) statement that outlines an organization's purpose.

Unsocial Media Management's mission statement is:

"To empower social media users to overcome the challenges that prevent them from discovering and leveraging the true potential of the internet."

For the record, I fully realize that your business's mission statement won't say anything about the way you're supposed to handle negative situations.

But if you were to write a mission statement about the specific harassment you're dealing with, would you rather it be "to argue with this person about his wrongdoing" or "to rise above the harassment and show the world a better way to respond"?

The main thing to remember is to maintain control of your focus rather than allowing the offender to gain control over you.

Why do You do What You do on Social Media?

Most business owners would say things like:

- To grow their audience.
- To educate new prospects on the benefits of their product or service.
- To build a more personalized relationship with clients, customers, and fans.

If you're having trouble coming up with good reasons why your business is (or should be) on social media, don't worry about it right now.

In Chapter Six, I'm going to show you some new ways to use social media that you've probably never thought about.

After seeing those, you'll probably come back to this chapter and make changes to your brand to align with your new vision.

In fact, you may decide to completely redefine the "who you are, what you do, and why you do what you do" on social media.

The Vision Statement

Once you've identified the main reasons why you and your business do what you do on social media, turn them into a vision statement.

A vision statement basically describes what you want your business to achieve in the future.

Written properly, a vision statement has the potential to create a "magnetic attraction" to what you want for your business.

Vision statements can be short and to the point, or they can be long and detailed, like a road map or a master plan.

A good example of an organization's vision is Habitat for Humanity's *"A world where everyone has a decent place to live."*

You can even write a vision statement when you notice something you don't like.

"A book that instills confidence in abused social media users."

This type of visualization is easy to do with practice. If you can get into the habit of looking at something you don't like and immediately turning your thoughts to something you'd rather see instead, you'll find it easy to write powerful vision statements that cause lasting change.

No matter how you come up with them, vision statements are great tools for keeping your company on track and helping you to prosper into the future.

Business "Like"

As you've already learned, smart businesses use a variety of tools and tactics to keep themselves on track. They know it doesn't pay to get involved in drama, so they do everything in their power to stay out of it.

Personal social media users could learn a lot from businesses. After all, most personal users don't use any tools at all to guide them through their online interactions.

The main reason for this is simple. Most personal social media users don't have goals. Businesses do. Serve the bottom line. That's it.

It would be easy to let emotion take over if you didn't have your bottom line to answer to. Luckily, you're in business. By staying in touch with who you are and what your goals are, you can easily understand how to manage social media interactions in a positive manner.

It won't matter if an attacker tries to bully you or not. You'll never fall victim to bad behavior when you're in touch with who you are and you keep your business goals in mind.

So make sure your social media goals fall in line with your business brand and your bottom line and keep them in front of you when negative people attack.

I promise they'll come in handy.

The Importance of Staying Focused

To understand how important it is to stay focused on your end goal, pretend you're a football player carrying the ball toward the end zone.

Now imagine that the harassment, negativity, and insults you encounter are the players from the other team trying to stop you.

If you were to focus on the opposing players instead of the goal line, you'd never score a touchdown. You'd be too busy butting heads with them to even remember where the end zone was at.

But that's exactly what you do when people make you mad on social media, isn't it? You argue, fuss, and fight instead of staying focused on your goals.

You allow them to take you off track and control your focus and energy.

Remember the hand-push lesson? Don't fall for it. Forget them and their drama. Focus on what you want for your business instead.

Let your goals and business focus guide your responses. Don't let negative comments derail you or your employees.

In Chapter 3: "The Authentic Response," you'll learn the right way to respond to an attacker's negative comments.

The Audience is Listening

It's easy to forget that everyone in your group or on your business page can see your conversations.

If you allow an attacker to steal your focus and cause you to respond out of character, you could say things that cause damage to your relationships with others who see the conversation.

When you're focused in a negative way on a bad situation, your ability to communicate effectively is diminished. You might say something you don't really mean, or you might not be as careful as you should, and say something negative about a person or group of people.

Don't allow anyone to cause you to say things you don't mean or wouldn't normally say on your own, as outlined in your business's social media policy.

Before you hit "post" or "publish," give some thought to who will see what you're about to say.

If your statement doesn't line up with your business's brand, take a step back, pause, and figure out something that better aligns with your image.

"Be" Someone Else

If you're having trouble mentally preparing yourself to deal with an attacker, there's a great strategy you can use to instantly feel more powerful.

Simply think of a person or business who would handle the situation well and imagine you're them when you communicate.

I'm not telling you to impersonate someone in a misleading way.

What I mean is that you can gain confidence by identifying with the strengths and mannerisms of people or businesses who handle certain situations better than you currently know how to.

This technique is called *assimilation*, and successful people have been using it for a long time.

For example, when I was a young skilled trades representative, I had to give a report in front of a group of 2,500 fellow representatives. I was scared stiff.

Luckily, I'd been taught about assimilation a couple weeks beforehand.

As I approached the podium, I imagined I was the President of our organization, an eloquent man who spoke clearly and powerfully.

I can't claim to have given the best speech at that gathering, but I did make it through my report without falling apart.

Although we normally think of assimilation as being something we do in person (such as a flight or combat simulator), it works incredibly well on social media too.

In fact, the ability to go back and see conversations on social media makes assimilation incredibly easy. By scrolling through old posts on walls and in groups, you can easily see if your "mentor" has already dealt with a similar situation and learn exactly how they handled it as it was happening.

Better Social Media

By now, I'm sure you're ready for me to stop telling you to focus on your brand and your goals before you even consider addressing a negative person's attack on social media.

But I can't place enough emphasis on the fact that answering in an emotional state puts the reputation of your business in jeopardy.

It's NEVER the right thing to do. I don't care what they say to (or about) you or your business. Don't ever let anyone's misbehavior cause you to act out of character.

Ok. I'll move on to the next talking point.

Have you ever heard that you get back what you put out?

Some people say it's the Law of Attraction. Some call it karma. Many just understand it without having to label it at all.

It's true. In life, you ultimately get back what you put out. More times than not, the way you treat others is reflected back to you.

And it's especially true on social media.

To have better social media, you have to put out better social media - even when a negative person attacks or harasses you.

I'll say it again in case you didn't quite catch it.

The key to getting back better social media is to put out better social media, regardless of how sad or angry an attacker's ugly comments make you feel.

I know it sounds like an impossible thing to do, but it's easier than you think. And now that you're properly prepared, you'll catch on quickly.

In Chapter 3, you'll learn how to give an authentic response when an attacker tries to throw you off course.

Let's get started.

CHAPTER 3

The Authentic Response

To set your business apart from the crowd on social media, learn to give an authentic response when someone harasses, attacks, or insults you.

You're thinking, "now you're telling me to give an authentic response back to the person who is *attacking* me?!? Isn't this a little overboard?"

I won't lie. At first, it won't be easy. Those old emotions will try to kick back in. You'll want to fight back. It's your natural instinct to do so.

But you'll get it right eventually. It's inevitable.

Once you've seen the process outlined below, you'll try it out from time to time in various situations. And you'll see (and feel) the difference between responding authentically and responding like you always have.

Let's jump right in.

What is an Authentic Response?

The word "authentic" means genuine, original, not false or copied.

So, in terms of Unsocial Media Management, an authentic response means you communicate from your (your business's) unique perspective in a way that sets you apart from everyone else.

The style in which you'll do this depends entirely on your brand, but the end-goal is the same for every business.

Respond with better social media in mind.

That's what an authentic response is.

An authentic response is a genuine, appreciative, compassionate reply that looks for common ground, lifts your attacker up, and respects their unique opinion and perspective.

I know this will feel hard to do initially; it almost feels like you'll be going against your better judgment. But hang in there. You'll understand how and why to do it by the end of the chapter.

Why Be Authentic?

It's pretty simple to understand actually. The person attacking you probably isn't your target audience, or even someone you'd like to influence who lines up with your brand.

This person just wants to be a pain in the butt, run your business down, and steal your energy. Don't let them get away with it. Use this opportunity wisely.

Do you remember in the *Introduction* when I told you "There's no better 'hook' than live drama" and that **everyone** pays attention when it happens?

Remember this and trust me. The people who matter to you the most are paying attention too. Drama gets noticed (that's why mass media puts it in front of you every day).

People like a "good fight." Remember back in high school when someone would yell "Fight!" and everyone would drop what they were doing to rush over and see what was going down? People are attracted to the drama and excitement that comes with conflict.

Unfortunately, a lot of people have come to expect everyone to be rude and disrespectful to one another on social media these days. But what they don't expect is for you to give an authentic response when someone is being rude to you or your business.

That will be a surprise to everyone, especially the person attacking you.

The people who have known you the longest will be intrigued and want to know what happened to you. Drama (good or bad) attracts attention!

Remember those harassing posts that used to make you cringe before you learned you could manage *unsocial media*? Those will soon be looked on as opportunities by everyone, once their eyes are opened to how to deal with it.

So use this opportunity to lead by example. Put your best social media foot forward and show your audience something great. Show them something they aren't expecting to see.

Show the world what authentic businesses do.

What Authentic Businesses Do

Authentic businesses strive to be **pleasantly unique**, even when drama slaps them up alongside the head.

How?

They consider that the person giving them a hard time could be going through a rough patch in life.

They look for common ground by focusing appreciatively on similar interests.

Authentic businesses make sure their message is clearly stated and easy to understand so it can't be taken the wrong way.

They admit they're not perfect and are thankful for the chance to learn from another's perspective. They appreciate criticism (even if it's not "constructive") because they know they could still learn from it.

Authentic businesses believe there's something good in everyone and strive to evoke it whenever they interact. They're good at breaking down the barriers that get in the way of **respectful communication,** which should always be the end goal.

They listen carefully and seize every opportunity to lift others up, especially the negative people who need it the most.

Authentic businesses genuinely want others to be well.

You're probably saying to yourself "That's not me - or my business."

Swallowing your pride is one thing, but caving in and catering to some jerk who said bad things about your product, business, or CEO is another.

But here's what you need to remember: The person harassing you is not the reason you're being authentic. The reason you're doing it is because you understand that putting out better social media will pay you back in better social media.

Remember, your target audience (and your competition) is paying attention. Communicate with them in mind. Treat your attacker as respectfully as you would treat your grandma.

Show your audience that you can still maintain control when your buttons are being pushed. Practice it in your personal life.

Before long it will be easy to leverage negativity to show the world that you are a powerful social media influencer.

Eventually, you won't have to deal with drama at all because you'll be getting back what you put out, essentially training your followers and your audience to communicate respectfully and authentically.

Before we go over specific examples of what authentic businesses do in 'unsocial media' situations, let's look at what authentic businesses DON'T do.

What Authentic Businesses Don't Do

It doesn't matter if you've done every single thing on the "What Authentic Businesses Do" list, it can all be wiped out in seconds if you don't pay attention to what authentic businesses DON'T do...

- They don't call the offender out or force them to defend their comment, opinion, or point of view.

- They don't send private messages or make remarks to others that contradict the things they've said in the group or on their business page.
- They don't use fear or negativity to try to make their point.
- They don't comment before they've checked their emotions and considered the message they're about to put out from many different perspectives.
- They don't allow their focus to be redirected from their business goals.
- They don't allow anyone to influence them to act out of character.
- They don't respond in an emotional state no matter what was said. (This is easy now that you understand the "hand-push" lesson from Chapter 1.)
- They don't manipulate or divide.
- They aren't flighty, unreliable, or negative.

Keep this list close by as a reminder when you're learning how to respond authentically. Taking time to look it over before you answer will help lower the risk of giving negative emotional responses when unsocial media strikes.

Seven Authentic Examples of How to Respond to Unsocial Media

Now that you know what it means to give an authentic response to an attack on your business on social media, let's explore some specific examples so you've got a better idea of the true definition of an authentic response.

Obviously, there's no way I could possibly cover every unsocial situation that could happen to you. The world is just too creative for me to try to list them all.

Besides, you know your business better than anyone and have probably already thought up some perfectly authentic responses to the type of drama you normally encounter.

But just in case you're caught up in a situation you can't figure out (or you just need some inspiration), below are seven examples of ways to handle online attacks. Feel free to adapt them to your situation or style. They won't work in every scenario, but if nothing else, they'll give you a better idea of what an authentic response really is.

#1: Appreciate their passion for the subject

Have you noticed some of the crazy things people will say to defend their opinion? Where do they come up with the energy to fight their battles? What made them so mad at your product, service, or business that they spend time focusing so much (negative) energy on you?

How did you get so lucky??

It's important to understand that the experiences we have in life fuel our passions, both positive and negative. If someone is expending a lot of energy to bring you down, acknowledge that they seem driven toward their cause and that you respect their level of intensity. You might even ask what drives them.

From there, you could compare their energy to your own drive and then lead the conversation into the reasons why you feel the way you do. This creates the expectation of an intelligent exchange of information. If they don't follow suit, their power diminishes.

When you acknowledge an adversary's power (momentum, drive, or energy), it's almost like you're a General standing on a hill looking down upon the force to be reckoned with. Even if the person in question isn't really powerful, you're shining a spotlight on their enthusiasm and drive and using it to your advantage.

When your target audience sees you acknowledging an attack in this confident manner, you'll give the impression that you're in control of the situation and that you're able to harness this energy.

A few years back, I actually told an attacker in a forum that I wished more of the people on my side were as driven as he was. I also told his allies that they were lucky to have him. They didn't like me telling them that, even though I didn't mean to offend them. Some people are never happy no matter what you do.

He tried to terrorize me for months after that, but his attempts were half-hearted and unsuccessful. I sort of treated him as a big brother would treat his misguided (yet formidable) younger brother, and he was angry with me for acting as if I knew him well.

Sometimes Unsocial Media Management can be fun.

Who knew you could take control of (or deflate) someone's drive and enthusiasm by publicly acknowledging their drive and enthusiasm?

#2: Respect their opinion and perspective

When you run into controversial subjects on social media, remember that there are reasons why people feel so strongly about certain issues. We tend to dismiss opinions when they don't match up with ours, but we shouldn't always do that.

Verbally respecting your attacker's opinion and perspective is another way to use their energy to your advantage.

You may think this is going too far (in terms of time and resources) when someone is bullying you, but again...you are not doing it for the bully.

Who knows? Some of the other people watching may partially feel the same way as that person, and it might benefit you to display an understanding of their reasoning.

In fact, there is a lot to be gained by learning to appreciate a controversial subject from the perspective of others. Don't be shy. Try to understand their reasons, and show them that you do by expressing appreciation for their passion and perspective.

(You'll learn in Chapter 7 that this is a key 'energy management' technique.)

It's easy to look at another person and find something you disagree with. That's what most people have been conditioned to do. Some even do it when they're not being harassed.

But if you give this type of positive response to a verbal attack, you'll instantly stand out from the crowd in a refreshing way. Not only did you not strike back or defend yourself, you gave your audience something unexpectedly positive.

It's almost like verbal judo, where you gain (perceived) power by showing that you can be bigger than their insult and instantly try to appreciate and understand them for their unique point of view.

This isn't easy to do, and it doesn't work in every situation, but believe me - you'll have plenty of opportunities to apply this technique if you spend enough time interacting on social media.

And who knows? You might consider changing your own opinion on the matter if the information is convincing enough. Respect the facts. It shows a lot of character to admit when you're wrong, and people will forgive and respect you for doing so.

If it happens, thank them for the information and show appreciation for setting you straight, even if they attacked you. You can even show enthusiasm for being free from the misinformation that had been holding you back.

But even if your standpoint on the issue doesn't change because of their perspective, you can still show respect for their point of view and their drive.

Be clear that you understand their opinion and thank them for the opportunity to understand the issue from another's unique perspective.

#3: Edify them for their strengths

In one forum I was in, a "radical" discounted every single thing I said and backed it with links to articles that (sort of) supported his point of view. He was very good at linking up information, he had a knack for graphics, he was good at writing headlines that got attention, and his points were short and well-constructed.

Don't get me wrong, he wrote things about me that didn't make me feel very good when I read them, and his 'facts' weren't accurate, well-informed, or well-intentioned.

How did I handle this? For one, I didn't ever let anyone think it bothered me. As we continued to communicate, I held my position but started to point out his strengths in communication, technology, and graphics.

In other words, it didn't even occur to me to stoop to his level (again, I know this is easier said than done, but it gets easier with practice).

He wasn't an easy egg to crack, but one day he brought up an issue that we both agreed was wrong and I seized the opportunity to help him. Together we brainstormed ideas on how to create social media posts and links to articles that supported our cause.

It had finally worked. By edifying his strengths, I had not only neutralized his negativity, I'd let him know that if the opportunity ever arose to work together on a project we agreed on, I would welcome the opportunity.

I set the stage beforehand, and it worked.

I can't say we're close buddies to this day, but I can tell you that we respect one another enough to listen to reason and come to agreements that help us both. And I appreciate his expertise in information and technology, which he still teaches me from time to time.

#4: Find Common Ground

When I was a young millwright on the factory floor, I was bumped from first shift (days) to the graveyard shift. I had worked day shift on the same day I was to report to third shift, and hadn't gotten a wink of sleep. I was dead tired when I walked into the plant.

At 3:30 am, I sat down to eat my lunch and fell asleep face down at the break table. Fifteen minutes after lunch was over, my new boss came to inform me that he had tried paging me twice for a breakdown that had happened right after lunch. When I looked at my pager, I saw it was true.

It was completely my fault, and my boss made it clear to me that he would not be giving me another chance before writing me up. I never fell asleep again. I did a lot of work and cleaned our department to keep myself awake.

I did my job well, and he knew it.

But the guy wouldn't give me a break. For months, he rode me and treated me poorly, even though I fixed everything he needed me to and excelled at my job.

When spring hit that year in Michigan, I was finally able to ride my Harley Davidson motorcycle to work again after a long winter. As I pulled my bike into the motorcycle parking, my boss pulled up alongside me on this sweet pearl white full dressed Harley with a matching sidecar. His white helmet and matching handlebar mustache were the toppings on the cake, and I couldn't help but smile and nod at him.

That night, he approached me in the break area, and we talked about motorcycles all through lunch and almost every night after that. Through getting to know him better, I discovered that he had just lost his wife to cancer and his mother was in rough shape, too. He said that his life at home had been rough and that he was sorry for taking it out on me.

I became friends with him, all because he saw that I liked the same brand of motorcycle as he did. If I'd pulled up on a Honda, he probably would have continued to mistreat me, even if I did smile at his matching pearly white ensemble.

Should I have gotten an attitude with him for being shallow and only approaching me after he saw my motorcycle? I'm glad I didn't do that. It wouldn't have solved my problem or resulted in that friendship.

And for the record, he later admitted that he'd seen me sleeping at lunchtime that first night and had paged me the minute it was over without needing to because there had been no breakdown. I still give him a hard time about that today.

Today's social media makes it simple to find common ground with virtually anyone. When you can scroll through their news feed, their profile, and their conversations with others, it's easy to discover common interests.

This makes social media an extremely powerful communication tool.

Even if you disagree with another person on almost every issue across the board, you can STILL find things you have in common if you're willing to look for them. Even if you have to get as basic as "we all have the spark of life inside us..."

Common ground is fertile soil for growing relationships.

#5: Be openly compassionate
A woman I used to work with had a bad habit of always arguing with me in social media forums for union business. She would not give me a break.

In one instance, she accused me of going out to lunch with Management, lying to the members about the details of a contract, and doing dishonest things while representing the members of our union. This nonsense went on for years!

After she had retired, she stayed in all those forums and continued to beat me up. I continued to be nice to her, always trying to maintain an authentic response.

One day, I heard through the grapevine that something horrible had happened in her family. She had lost a grandson to an incurable disease.

I sent her a heartfelt private message wishing her and her family strength and peace, and she messaged me back very quickly and told me about a few other tough things that had recently happened in her life.

I listened to her struggles, gave my best advice, and wished her well.

Not long after that happened, one of her friends started to tear me apart on a post I'd written in a group forum, and she (this person who used to do the same) came to my rescue.

After that incident had been resolved, she wrote a long post in that same forum telling all the others that she'd been wrong about me all those years and that I'd always tried to help her, no matter how rotten she'd been to me.

I have to say, there's a LOT of power when you can convert a critic into not only a fan but someone who would defend your name when you're not around to do it yourself.

I totally believe that being compassionate to her, regardless of how she treated me, was key in her complete turnaround.

When she apologized, I made sure to tell her that I understood her being upset because I knew there were issues and forces at work that were not fair to her, yet I had no control over any of it.

When you use compassion to guide your responses and understand that there might be other things going on in their lives that you might not be aware of, it's easier to stick to respectful communication in the face of their attacks. You also leave the line open for a complete turnaround, like I had with the sweet little lady mentioned above.

#6: Be Willing to Give a "Pass"

"LIFE IS 10% WHAT HAPPENS TO US AND 90% HOW WE REACT TO IT." — CHARLES R. SWINDOLL

If someone were to cut you off in traffic, slam on their brakes, and make a painfully slow left-hand turn in front of you, how would you react?

Would you grind your teeth and shake your head? Would you get mad and lay on the horn? Would you do all of the above and then turn in behind them to give them a piece of your mind?

What if you did just that and discovered that it was your grandma or your favorite teacher from school? How quickly would your reaction change then?

We give people "passes" depending on who they are all the time.

How many times has a member of your family made a political statement that you disagree with?

You might not agree with your grandma's driving or politics, but you love her apple pie and would certainly do anything for her.

Get better at giving people passes on social media. Try turning the other cheek more often.

But how do you do that with someone who is constantly coming after you and your business online?

Remember, authentic businesses respond with the other person's well-being in mind.

What if you found out later that giving them a 'pass' helped them through a tough time? Wouldn't you rather have a fan for life than someone who is always out to get you?

#7: Ask for suggestions/solutions

Have you ever noticed how some people are very quick to tell you why your business ideas won't work, but they rarely propose viable solutions to the problem?

I ran into that problem a lot when trying to help manage change into an evolving workforce, and I was inspired to develop some strategies to help move things along.

One of my favorite strategies was to subtly suggest multiple ideas for change to an operator or someone working in the affected area. Rather than try to force the change I really wanted, I'd drop hints or suggest that a change might be beneficial.

Later, I'd talk about that same issue and congratulate them for their great idea. Before you knew it, the change I thought was best was implemented with little resistance.

The reason this works is that people are more open to change if they believe it's their idea. If they feel they have skin in the game, they'll get on board.

This strategy can also work well in online conversation. In fact, you can plant the seed of an idea and extract it back out with buy-in in a very short amount of time if you understand the concept.

Another option is that after you've told a negative person that you respect their opinion, go ahead and ask for their ideas to resolve the problem.

By respectfully inviting their input, you're opening the door to discuss the factors surrounding an issue.

As your audience sees you staying on topic and communicating respectfully, they'll be more likely to offer their own opinion when a topic they're interested in comes up.

Choose to 'shut this person down,' and you're essentially slamming the door in your audience's face, which makes them feel that they can't speak up when an important issue comes up.

Some companies fully realize how valuable their employees' ideas are, and they've created suggestion programs to improve their operations. Some even make a show of reading out the best suggestions at employee meetings and make sure to implement at least a few each month.

On your company's social media marketing page, you could mention that you're open to reviews of your products and services, whether they're positive or negative. If you express that you're open to ideas and criticism from the people who use your products in the real world, you're inviting feedback that can be used to make your business better.

Tell your customers that you appreciate their feedback and use it to make your company better every day.

Now it's Your Turn

The ideas mentioned above won't fit every situation you'll encounter. In fact, you could probably write your own book of ideas on how to respond authentically to negativity, harassment, and drama for your business.

Remember, responding authentically is about focused appreciation. If you can discover something that your attacker likes, you can then focus appreciation on their love of that thing, and you have a better chance of making a positive connection.

The whole key to 'breaking' these tough people down (so they don't feel like an enemy) is to find common ground and be willing to give respect, even if they are wrong.

If you want to be a powerful social media influencer, you have to be different. Social media has become pretty negative these days. If you can create a good-feeling place where people know they'll be treated with compassion and respect, your business will reflect that change in a positive way.

You can also use authentic responses in your employee communications that make them feel more valued, make them feel more secure in their jobs, or improve their attitude in some way.

But what happens when you try everything you can think of to be authentic, and it doesn't make a difference at all? Are you just meant to 'suck it up' and ignore it?

No. In the next chapter, you'll learn what to do when all else fails.

Turn the page to find out more.

CHAPTER 4

If the Gloves Must Come Off

*[**NOTE**: Although some of you might be tempted to skip right to this chapter because someone won't quit harassing you, please know that these tactics won't work without understanding the ideas that led up to this point. Although I understand your frustration (believe me, **I DO!**), please go back and at least skim through the subheads in each chapter.]*

Now then.

Sometimes, no matter how nice or authentic you try to be, it still isn't enough to get an angry person to leave you alone. In these situations, it pays to know how to put a stop to their nonsense before you resort to blocking or reporting them.

If you block negative people too quickly or regularly ban them from your page, you'll gain a reputation as being someone who doesn't allow Freedom of Speech. Your business doesn't need a reputation like that.

Although you're only trying to keep communication respectful and protect your business, blocking and banning normally backfires.

Most of the time, they're the ones violating *your* Freedom of Speech, but they'll always say otherwise.

Once kicked off your page, they'll go into other groups (or worse - on your competitor's pages) and twist the details of the story to turn every audience against you.

They'll capture a screenshot of that time they pushed your buttons just right and leave it as a photo comment when you call them out for bad behavior. They'll leave negative comments on articles, blog posts, and other review sites, and there won't be much you can do about it.

Trying to defend your position against their endless banter is pointless. Interacting with them on their level at all is a race to the bottom.

But you need to get them to stop. It's time for the gloves to come off.

Again, these tactics are ONLY to be used after you've put the information in the first three chapters to use. If you've given your all in front of your audience, you've most likely endeared them to your situation, so they'll understand your change of direction.

In fact, some of your supporters may have sent private messages asking why you don't just bounce the bully. (That exact thing happened to me several times when I was a negotiator.)

If that happens, send them a message back saying that we're all God's children or explain that the negative person is probably going through a hard time or something and thank them for their concern.

Make sure you're as authentic in private as you are in public.

Let the Air Out

To get an attacker to abandon their campaign and walk away, **diffuse their energy by deflating their ego**.

As you well know, I don't condone pushing back against someone's negative energy. It's contrary to what I've taught you thus far. That being said, sometimes you have to take a different approach and focus more on putting a stop to drama, harassment, and insults.

And technically, these ideas aren't about pushing back - but they're not exactly about being nice either. They're merely an attempt to get your offender to leave you alone by pointing out a few things they may not have thought about...

In reality, it's all about managing energy.

#1: There is no Better Hook Than Live Drama

As we discussed previously, live drama gets attention. It's why the news is full of it, and it's also the reason why 'the media' creates it on a daily basis. (In their defense, they say their ratings indicate that people want drama and controversy...)

We've already established that you can endear your target audience by responding authentically to a negative attack. When your goal is to build a positive relationship with your customers, followers, fans, or employees, an authentic response is the right choice 99% of the time.

But there's another way to use this drama to your advantage.

As I told you before, one of the first lessons I learned in copywriting school was that good marketing requires a powerful "hook" to grab your audience's attention.

And live drama *is* the best way to get attention.

So, if you think about it just right, you'll realize that your attacker is actually doing your business a huge favor by harassing you and getting your target audience's attention.

You should thank them. Publicly.

And after you do, you should go on to tell them why you're so happy with their actions.

Let them know that since they first went out of their way to harass you, you've been able to create a better bond with your target audience by being authentic in the face of their misbehavior.

(Make it clear that it's who you are and you don't plan to stop.)

They provided you with a unique opportunity to stand out from your competition. You could never have displayed how genuine you were unless this attacker had given you the chance.

Thank them.

They also helped you to understand how to grow yourself personally by figuring out how to overcome a challenging situation. (Some people would pay big bucks for this sort of training.)

And be careful not to seem ungrateful for all their hard work. After all, it's not easy to mount a good attack. A proper assault requires time, dedication, and emotion. Don't overlook their sacrifice. They deserve recognition. Appreciate them for their effort.

They've done a lot for you. Don't you think you should at least thank them for playing such a prominent role in your social media marketing success?

Tell them that their nonstop nonsense has helped you to boost your business's reach and expand your audience. Let them know that others in the group have been privately pulling for you, and thank them for helping you create more personalized relationships.

And when they completely lose their temper and resort to blowing up your thread by commenting 73 times in a row, tell them:

#2: "Thanks for Boosting My Posts"

Most people won't read through a hundred comments on a business post, but your original post will show up more frequently in your target audience's feed when an attacker keeps it alive by commenting multiple times.

It's the way social media works. As more people show an interest in a post, it pops up in more people's feeds every time a comment is added. So every time a negative person tries to drag you down by leaving a comment, they're actually boosting your original post.

So again, thank them for it.

And if they try to say that you're incorrect and everyone and their brother is still hanging on every word, thank them again, this time for...

#3: Helping You to Communicate the Details

Every time someone calls you out on an aspect of your product, service, or business, it gives you the chance to share more of your features and benefits with your target audience.

As your attacker tries to discredit your business with negative tactics and misinformation, it gives you the chance to publicly display the finer details of your organization or offering.

Very few marketing tools can accomplish such in-depth communication. Your assailant is probably doing a better job at educating your fans than your marketing team.

"It almost feels like I should pay you..."

The bottom line is if you can convince your attacker that their efforts are actually helping you rather than hurting you, they will eventually lose interest and take their drama elsewhere.

Their goal is to steal your focus by getting you to push back against them, but you're too smart for that. Let their attack go right past you and immediately turn the tables by showing them how you've harnessed their energy to use it to your advantage.

Again, these are only three examples of how to diffuse their energy and deflate their ego. You <u>can</u> and <u>will</u> come up with your own techniques that fit your situation and solve your problem.

Tools, Tips, and Tactics

If none of these copywriting tactics work and the negative person is still going strong, an alternative option is to use the available tools provided by the social media platform you're on. These include blocking, unfollowing, or reporting the offender.

There are also some apps that help you to manage your social media accounts in a more powerful way, and new books, tools, techniques, and information are conceptualized and released every day.

By this point, everyone will completely understand your decision to move past the drama. They've probably grown as tired of it as you have. They may even step up to defend your name in other forums if they see your bully trying to run you down after you were so nice to them for so long.

Take a Stand

It's important to put a stop to online bullying whenever you have the chance to do so.

Don't be afraid to stand up for others who are being abused in your group or on your fan page. You now know more about managing online drama than 99% of social media users. Put your knowledge to good use.

As a business, you should step up whenever the opportunity presents itself. If you're the group administrator or page owner, remove the offending person and reach out to the person being bullied to offer them your support.

If you don't control the forum or group where the bullying is happening, contact the forum administrator for help or seek help from the social media provider if things are getting out of control.

If you're out of ideas, try calling in a professional Unsocial Media Manager or posting your problem in the Unsocial Media Management for Business Facebook forum here https://www.facebook.com/Unsocial-Media-Management-1662671000675974/.

Now it's time to move on to the future of social media in regard to your business. Turn the page to get started.

CHAPTER 5

Social Media and the Future of Your Business

Even after reading this far, you might still be on the fence about whether social media is right for your business.

For starters, dealing with negative people is no fun. It's even worse if social media isn't "your thing."

Then there's the investment of time, money, and human resources.

And we've all heard the story about the reputation of a business being damaged because of social media.

So why even bother with it?

Here to Stay

If there's one thing I can tell you for sure, it's that social media isn't going to disappear. Businesses aren't going to stop using it. Neither are personal users. It's ingrained into their lives, even if it appears to be mostly negative at times.

Truthfully speaking, most business owners couldn't get away from social media if they tried. Regardless of whether you create a social media presence or not, your company will still end up on review sites, blogs, podcasts, or anywhere else people can post or leave a comment.

Left unanswered, negative feedback can damage your bottom line. It's in your best interest to learn how to deal with it and take control of your social media presence.

Times Are Changing

There's a lot going on in the world today. The climate for business can change in a hurry.

Companies can really take a beating as the economy adjusts to new government policies, globalization, changing health care costs, and a host of other unpredictable challenges.

We all know what happens when businesses can't adapt to change. One day you're profitable. The next you're bankrupt...

For companies to navigate these challenging times, they must be able to quickly and effectively manage change throughout the business.

But as you learned in the hand-push lesson in Chapter One, most people are resistant to change. They push back if they don't understand or agree with why change is necessary.

The best companies at adapting to change place a high value on creating and maintaining respectable two-way communication with their workforce.

To achieve this goal, they're turning to social media.

Good managers realize the importance of everyone at every level understanding and (if possible) supporting the reasons for change, or their efforts won't be as effective.

They know their employees and suppliers are already using social media. There's no training or special website needed. Placing a message directly in the palm of their workers' hands (even when they're not at work) is as simple as asking them to join a page or a group.

Social Media's "Coming of Age"

In the big scheme of things, social media is a relatively new way to communicate. Although people have been talking to one another in person for thousands of years, most of the social media channels we use today are just over a decade old.

And social media has improved a **lot** since it first came out. You might not remember all the updates, but trust me - you'd grow frustrated very quickly if you had to use the first version of your favorite app.

In roughly ten years, social media has evolved from an awkward college communication experiment into an easy-to-use application that empowers you to comfortably interact with almost anyone you choose on any topic you can think of.

And whether you realize it or not, social media is communication *technology*.

Have you ever heard that a computer is considered "outdated" six months after you buy it? Wouldn't it make sense that online communication technology would be directly influenced by improvements in computer technology?

It's true. Never before in history has any method of communication grown as rapidly or as powerfully as today's social media. Technologically speaking, it grows smarter, leaner, and faster with each passing moment.

(*It's definitely matured faster than most of the people who use it.*)

It's learning about you, too. It knows what you like and dislike...

Have you ever searched for a product or service and immediately noticed that similar ads start to pop up on your social media homepage or in your newsfeed?

That's because it's all linked on the web, and it's getting to know YOU.

It's also getting to know your clients, employees, customers, fans, and prospects and what *they* like and dislike. (That's HUGE from a marketing standpoint! More on this opportunity in Chapter Seven.)

Although there are several more reasons why social media is a good investment for today's businesses, there's one reason that towers above all the rest.

If it's alright with you, I'll just skip to that one right now...

The Conceptual Age

The timing is absolutely perfect.

Social media could not have come along at a better moment in history.

The global economy has entered the Conceptual Age. In simple terms, this means that today's biggest economic opportunities are based in ideas, information, and concepts.

Can you think of a better tool for sharing ideas and developing concepts with like-minded people? Social media's unique strengths make it absolutely perfect for the job at hand.

But not everyone understands the economic "shift" into this Conceptual Age. For example, a lot of today's job seekers are still trying to land traditional jobs like their parents or grandparents did.

In my opinion, they're wasting their time. Those old jobs aren't as lucrative or as plentiful as they once were. In fact, today's economy isn't the same (for job seekers **or** businesses) as it was even a decade ago, let alone when grandpa was a young man.

The internet has completely changed things. Some of those old professions are never coming back. Many people are disappointed to hear this news, but it's not the end of the world - it's the beginning of a new era.

You see, the opportunity to prosper isn't gone, it's just shifted to a different economic sector.

The sooner you understand this, the sooner you can capitalize on it. After all, this isn't the first time the economy has undergone a major transition. The same thing has happened several times over the last hundred years. Each new transition provided an opportunity to learn new lessons.

The period before the 1930's was known as the **Agricultural Age.** During that time, most of the workforce was dedicated to farming to produce enough food for the entire population.

But as big farm equipment and advancing agricultural technology came along, small farmers were forced to either transition into bigger operations or quit farming for a living.

Many displaced farmers chose to go to work in the new factories that were built as the economy transitioned out of the Agricultural Age and into the **Industrial Age**.

Industry grew strong and changed the world quite a bit from the 1940's to the early 1990's. After that, many factories were hit hard by globalization, cheap labor, and economic recession.

About the time industry started to falter, the internet went mainstream. This period was quickly named the **Information Age** because people made money when others accessed the information they'd uploaded online.

But that didn't last long either, and the economy took a huge hit when the tech bubble burst and caused the dot.com crash. Because of that whole mess, some people swore off the internet as a source of income. (Big mistake, in my opinion.)

We've now arrived at the **Conceptual Age**, where ideas and information are combined, packaged, and delivered to the people, businesses, and other entities that consume them.

Are you beginning to understand why I feel that the people still seeking traditional professions could be making better use of their time?

Don't get me wrong, I'm well aware that there are still some pockets of prosperity in agriculture, industry, and information.

In fact, the Conceptual Age is causing significant change in those areas as well.

But it doesn't pay to spend time looking for opportunity where it used to be.

Making a Monkey Out of the Middleman

If you take a look around, you'll see examples of the Conceptual Age economy everywhere.

For example, the *concept* of shopping from home is fully responsible for the change in retail over the last decade or so. Think about how many shopping malls and retail stores have closed lately. Those jobs aren't coming back.

Retail shopping has evolved from a brick and mortar experience to online ordering and home (or anywhere) delivery in three clicks or less from wherever you're at.

The world didn't know what to think when this concept was first introduced. Some people resisted, claiming they liked the experience of going shopping and that they wanted to touch their merchandise before they bought it.

The newer generations don't seem to care as much. They like the convenience of 'buying in one click' from their phone and having their purchases show up on their doorstep more than they enjoy the experience of shopping.

And because they're buying online and there's no "middle man" (retailer), they can get a lower price on the same items.

This fact alone has caused many who had previously resisted online shopping to give it a try. Most don't look back after they realize they're getting a great deal on store-quality merchandise without having to fight a crowd or leave the comfort of their home. They've grown to like that it frees up time in their busy lives.

Although I used this specific example because most people can understand the change in retail, trust me when I say that retail is just one small slice of our overall economic pie. Concepts are changing the business landscape in **every** sector of the economy.

In some cases, outdated jobs are being eliminated, combined, or otherwise replaced. In others, high-tech or otherwise advanced opportunities are being created where there was previously no opportunity at all.

Will social media, the Conceptual Age, and today's changing economic landscape make a monkey out of your business?

Change is going to happen whether you accept it or not. One thing's for sure - with the recent trend toward buying direct, it doesn't appear to be the right time to set your sights on becoming a middleman.

The way this new age will affect your ability to prosper will depend on the nature of your business, the way you perceive new ideas and technology, and whether or not the world wants/needs what you have to offer.

In the next chapter, we'll check out some great examples of how social media and the Conceptual Age are being put to work in the world of business.

Are you ready to check out some ideas that work?

CHAPTER 6

Ideas that Work

Ideas make businesses better, faster, and easier to run.

Ideas save work, time, and resources.

Ideas improve processes. Ideas expand businesses. Ideas pay the bills.

Ideas work. They actually do physical work.

Don't believe me?

Consider this: a robot was once someone's idea. There's no doubt that hundreds of thousands of robots are running at full speed at this very second all over the globe. Today's automotive manufacturers would be LOST without robots. In fact, every industry would.

And a robot is just **one** idea.

There are literally thousands of new business ideas emerging on a daily basis that combine social media with advancing technology, forward-thinking marketing methods, and new business concepts.

If you've checked out your competition's marketing tactics, I'm sure you've seen plenty of ways to use social media to promote your business or build your audience.

But you don't have to be like that other guy if you don't want to. If you've got a unique idea to connect with your target audience, BY ALL MEANS, try it out.

Because judging by all the cool things I've seen lately (my perspective may be different than yours because of the way I've been focused), I'm inclined to believe that almost anything is possible for smart businesses on social media.

And I want you to feel the same way.

With that in mind, I'd like to share a few key lessons I've learned as well as some great examples I've noticed. I'm truly impressed with the way some of today's smart business owners and managers are using social media in their day-to-day operations. I think you will be too.

My hope is that one or more of these examples resonates with you enough to get you to take action.

Because, once you gain the first-hand experience of ideas actually performing the work, you'll drop any inhibitions you have about ideas for change and your real business growth can begin.

How Successful Small Businesses Use Social Media

If you've been in business a while, you've probably noticed how some small business owners and managers use social media in their marketing and customer service efforts.

Many of them do it like this:

First, they get their target audience to "like" their business page through drawings, giveaways, or discounts on goods and services. After that, they focus on creating a personalized relationship with their "followers" through a variety of social media marketing methods.

By putting their company name and brand in front of their audience on a regular basis, they're creating comfort and familiarity by just showing up in their newsfeed regularly.

Some companies create informational posts designed to educate customers and prospects about current products or to create "hype" prior to the release of new ones. Others offer discounts on various holidays or specialized rates if you book a service in advance.

Many businesses regularly post links to articles related to their business that their target audience might find useful. Providing free and helpful information in this manner positions their business name or brand in front of their audience in a positive light.

There are literally thousands of ways to promote your business on social media. How you choose to do it depends on the nature of your business and your social media goals.

"I've Got a Guy for that…"

When I first started studying marketing, I helped a few friends promote their service businesses around the area we lived in. It didn't take long to learn an important lesson about how local people look at local small businesses.

When it comes to community-based small businesses, customers want to do business with someone they know and like.

It sounds simple, right? When it comes to local services, people want to feel "taken care of." They're willing to forego the "deal of the week" discount from *that other guy* because they value "**their guy's**" expertise and feel he truly represents their best interests.

If you use social media to establish a personalized relationship with your audience and create good working relationships with those you interact with, you'll become "their guy."

For example, I've purchased 7 of my last 8 vehicles through the same guy at a Chevy dealership over 30 miles away from my house. I drive past 4 other Chevy dealerships to get there, but I don't even consider going anywhere else.

I've got a guy for that.

I've been sold since he made me that first awesome car deal so many years ago. He treats me right every time. My guy takes care of all of my transportation needs. That's just the way it is.

He knows that loyalty is built on trust, respect, and excellent customer service. It's obvious that he really enjoys what he does, and I appreciate doing business with him. (He's now a top manager on a truly excellent team.)

In turn, I send him business and do whatever I can to promote his dealership.

When someone else tries to sell me a Chevy, I cut them off short and tell them "I've got a guy for that..."

Social media is a great tool for building the kind of personalized relationships that will have your followers thinking of your name every time they (or the people they talk to) need the service you provide. Be their guy.

A Sparkling Example

A friend of mine quit his factory job about five years ago to start his own power washing company. Many of our coworkers thought it was crazy for a 24-year-old guy with a young family to quit a job with benefits in a bad economy to go wash trucks and houses for a living.

He just smiled and told them he thought he could get ahead if he worked hard and was smart about the jobs he took. And he was right.

But it also didn't hurt that he managed his business in a conceptual way from the beginning.

My friend Dan is a very likable guy. He's good at customer service, and most people trust him right away. He knows the value of being "their guy," and he shows it by being personable, respectful, and doing an excellent job.

He built his business slowly at first, doing whatever it took to make sure his customers were satisfied. He paid for advertising and had his work trailer "wrapped" with his name and company information. He also had a website designed and created a Facebook business page.

As he grew, he continued to invest in training and new technology. He attended power washing seminars and took out a loan for a bigger truck with a specialized cleaning system that would allow him to command more money - IF he could book new business.

He did. He wrote letters for free wash jobs (demonstrations) to the managers of big trucking companies. He submitted proposals for specialized cleaning at various industrial facilities. He also put ads in the paper about preparing for your best summer yard by washing your house in April before your flowers begin to bloom.

This guy HUSTLED, but he was very smart with his time and focus.

He made sure his employees were up-to-date on the latest industrial standards, so there was no issue with any of them entering a facility and performing any task necessary. He successfully branded his business as an excellent company that provides a high-tech, environmentally-friendly service.

And he continued to grow and evolve.

One year, he planned his family vacation around a new technology seminar in Florida during spring break. The family hung out by the pool at the hotel while he went to class in the morning, then after about 1 pm, the vacation was ON...

When he came home, he was the proud owner of a brand-new (and very expensive) washing system designed for one specific task.

I have to admit, when he told me what it was for, I wasn't so sure he'd made a good investment...

Roof Wash Anyone?
I didn't know that Dan had purchased a new roof washing system when I called him up to have the siding

on my house washed. He casually scheduled the date and time and asked if I wanted to include a roof washing.

This caught me off guard, and I asked him "Why?"

He explained that dirt...not sun, winter, rain, nor wind...was the **number one** cause of shingle breakdown.

The next question I asked was "Wait... Doesn't power washing destroy shingles?"

He said that special solvents in the new soft wash systems are designed to interact with shingle components to gently get them to let go of dirt, so high pressure isn't necessary. The process also leaves behind a protective coating designed to prolong the life of the roof.

I'd never heard of soft roof washing technology before, but as I started to notice all the filthy rooftops around my neighborhood, I realized the market was ripe for the picking. He sent me a link to a quick video of the system in action, and I was more than impressed with the process and the before and after pictures.

After watching it, I sent him a text asking if he was booked solid for roof washes, and he told me "No, not at all. People aren't too interested." He said that the main problem was that most people don't think about washing the shingled roof of their house.

As I thought about it, I realized he was right. Where we live in Michigan, most people wash their houses once or twice a year, but washing our rooftop isn't something we normally do here. The rain does that, right?

Don't get me wrong, I've known people who had specific problems that could have been prevented by a good washing. When trees block the sun and drop debris on a rooftop, it can eventually cause mold if not cleaned off. Plus, I'd seen some pretty dirty roofs on newer houses in really nice neighborhoods, so it made sense that there was a market for washing roofs.

The problem around here was that most people didn't realize they *could* wash their roof. Those who had tried to wash mold or dirt off found out quickly that shingles weren't meant to be power washed.

Many people in these parts have simply accepted that they'll need to replace their shingled roof after 12-15 years instead of the 20 that's printed on the package.

After thinking it over a while, I offered to write an article to promote his new contraption. I titled it "Why 20-Year Shingles NEVER Last 20 Years."

(As it turns out, the elements *do* play a part in the deterioration of shingles, but not in the way you might think. Clean shingles are designed to expand and contract with extreme temperatures. The breakdown occurs when dirt gets in the cracks and doesn't allow the shingle materials to 'work' properly.)

To make a long story short, dirt is the reason why 20-year shingles never last 20 years.

Before long, several area homeowners who had never even thought about paying a professional to scrub their home's dome were shelling out big bucks to have a longer-lasting roof.

The visual marketing aspects took over from there. Everyone who saw the difference on their neighbor's house immediately wanted theirs done. Dan made it easy to contact him by leaving a yard sign (if the property owner agreed) or by coming back to the neighborhood the following day with roof washing flyers.

As a marketing guy, it occurs to me every time I think about this scenario that he created a market that wasn't available until he told them they needed it.

But he's good at what he does, and he's good at letting people know about it.

He owns other specialized cleaning systems as well, and he informs his target customers when new technology arrives that's better suited to their needs. His investment in new technology and the way he's branded himself as an expert have empowered him to command top dollar for his crew's time and effort.

Some of the other power washing companies around town aren't doing as well as Dan's company is. Many are trying to compete in the same economy using machines that are almost twenty years old. If you ask the owners of those companies about their economic outlook, they'll say it's hard to make a living these days.

Not Dan. Dan is pumped up about the future. He gets excited when it's time to try new power washing and marketing methods. He's not afraid to try new processes and invest in new technology, because he knows it has the potential to pay off big in the long run.

How Powerful Corporations Leverage Social Media

(Note: Despite the fact that this section was developed with large corporations in mind, many small business owners and managers have indicated that many of these techniques have proven useful in their day-to-day operations as well.)

Although large corporations use social media in many of the same ways as smaller businesses (marketing, customer service, special offers), I'm not going to waste time talking about the "normal" ways that big businesses leverage social media. Most of them have experienced marketing teams in place who are very good at what they do.

Instead, I'm going to share some cutting-edge ways that big businesses are leveraging social media to focus inwardly, on what (some people say) is the company's most valuable asset...the **employees**.

"CLIENTS DO NOT COME FIRST. EMPLOYEES COME FIRST. IF YOU TAKE CARE OF YOUR EMPLOYEES, THEY WILL TAKE CARE OF THE CLIENTS."
— RICHARD BRANSON

If you're a corporate manager, how does the above statement make you *feel*?

I'm not asking for the answer you'd give in front of a room full of people. I intentionally asked how it made you FEEL (inside).

Although many corporate managers would love to be able to put their employees (except maybe the lazy ones) first, aren't they still morally obligated to put shareholders and customers before employees?

But putting others before your employees doesn't put employees first anymore, does it?

Well, where does it put them? Third? Fifth?

Are they even on the *first page*??

My point is that many corporate (and manufacturing) employees don't feel as involved or appreciated as they'd like to. They feel like just a number. (And it's **not** number one!)

Some feel they face the same challenges day in and day out with no help from those who have the power and/or responsibility to remedy their situation. After a while, they start to care less about their own responsibilities, and there is a negative trickle-down effect.

In powerful organizations, employees feel they're an important part of the business.

They feel valued. They feel their efforts are appreciated. They feel good about their job.

They feel they come first.

So how do you close the gap from whatever number they're at to number one?

The answer is **communication**.

The key to closing the gap between employees who feel like just a number and ones who feel they come first is **regular and respectful two-way communication**.

While it's true that you have to communicate information to create understanding so changes are supported and effective, it's equally important for your workforce to be able to communicate back to you.

(For the record, good employees will never tell you they think they should come before the customer. They know it's not the way business works.)

But they DO want to feel appreciated, valued, and informed.

The best tool for achieving this goal is social media. (You might have predicted that I was going to say that.)

But it's true. Despite their past resistance to getting involved in social media, large corporations can see the writing on the wall. They know their employees aren't going to stand in front of a bulletin board to read company updates, but they *will* be scrolling through their newsfeed.

So they're meeting them where they're at.

From a corporate standpoint, social media provides an easy way to communicate with a massive workforce on a platform they're already trained to use.

They're using social media groups to put out company updates, post opportunities for job advancement, link to benefits information, announce company functions, give business updates, promote employee discount programs, and communicate other information designed to provide value to the workforce.

They're investing time and resources into social media campaigns, implementing updated policies on social media use, and reading books like this one to learn advanced methods of communicating.

They're making employees feel appreciated and letting them know that their opinion and business insights are valued enough to be taken into consideration.

Their goal is to become a positive, helpful, and familiar part of the employee's newsfeed.

They're no longer concerned about the negativity that held their efforts back in the past. They've learned that unsocial media is manageable. (At least most of them have.)

Some companies have implemented social media campaigns designed to get employees more involved in change around the workplace. They take the time to appreciate their involvement and show the same professionalism in giving authentic responses when they communicate with their workers as they would a client.

They do all this because they know they're making a significant investment in the **future** of their company.

A Solid Investment

In today's complex economy, large companies need to be flexible enough to weather the tough times yet bold enough to take advantage of opportunities for growth.

The ones that can quickly adapt to change are coming out on top.

With that in mind, it's easy to understand why any expert would advise businesses to put their employees first.

Your employees are in contact with your customers. They're ultimately responsible for quality and productivity. Employees are the face of your business and the drivers of your bottom line. They're on the front line. They're already first in a lot of respects.

Although this sounds like a great reason to invest in employee communications, it's not the biggest reason why companies are finally embracing social media. They've always known their employees were important.

The reason they're embracing change **now** is for an entirely different reason altogether...

Do you remember when I pointed out that computer technology and communication technology are intertwined and advancing at a similar (rapid) pace?

Do you know what's also happening at the same time?

Because of advancing communication technology, **communication itself** *is rapidly evolving.*

In other words, new technology is training the user and bringing them up to speed.

Along with that, people are starting to discover ways around the drama and negativity that had previously held them back.

Apps are being created that empower users to manage their newsfeeds in new and exciting ways while eliminating negative influences like politics and mass media drama. Books like this one are being regularly released that are specifically geared toward improving the online communication experience.

Better social media is trending.

That's right. People are getting smarter. They figured out how to 'use' their favorite social media app a long time ago, but now they're learning how to *communicate*.

Smart companies are taking advantage of this momentum and helping their workers improve their communication skills as they learn to evolve themselves. They know it's in their best interest to be right there on the leading edge of this transformation with their employees.

They realize there's a huge amount of untapped potential inside their workforce. (Possibly up to 90% in some cases, as you'll learn in the next chapter.)

They know that to take advantage of this extraordinary opportunity, they'll need to invest time, money, and other resources. Most don't have a problem with this because they understand it will benefit their business in the long run.

Powerful corporations already know all about the Conceptual Age. Many had to drastically change their business model to survive when new concepts changed the economic landscape around them. Others found great prosperity in the economic shift to new and improved processes.

All of them learned the value of good ideas.

The biggest lesson many of them learned is that in today's evolving economy, ideas for transforming the business can come from anywhere.

That's why they're leaving no stone unturned.

They know that if they can train their employees to look for opportunities to improve the business and convince them to share their unique ideas, the company will prosper.

They understand that new ideas and concepts are worthwhile investments that have the potential to pay off big.

How big?

The Million Dollar Idea

If you could invest $20,000 and get a GUARANTEED $100,000 in return, would you?

I tried to get my tech guys to design a virtual hand that popped out and smacked anyone who answered "No," but the technology isn't quite there yet.

(At the rate this world is advancing, it won't be long before someone figures it out.)

But seriously, anyone would make this deal if they could.

Some smart businesses make this deal every day. It's called a suggestion program.

A suggestion program is a way for companies to invest in the ideas their employees have for improving the business.

Employees can write suggestions to save money or increase profits, improve safety, and address any number of operational issues.

Ideas for savings include (but are not limited to):

- Cost reduction
- Safety improvements
- Energy savings
- Labor savings
- Better processes
- Advancing technology
- Waste reduction
- Quality improvements
- Scrap reduction
- Communication improvements
- Process simplification

Most suggestion programs pay a portion (usually 10-25%) of the overall (twelve-month) savings to the employee(s) responsible for coming up with the idea, but only you can decide what pay structure works best for your business.

There are several reasons why implementing a suggestion program is a good idea.

For one, it's money in the bank. Suggestions aren't paid out until after the company has verified that the idea is valid and useful.

Many times, large payouts are made in installments. Once the company has verified that the savings have made the business more profitable over a given period of time (again, usually a year), they pay the remainder of the balance.

Another reason suggestions work so well is that employees are less resistant to change if something is their idea. We've already discussed how resistant some people are to change, but when it's their idea and they stand to make a profit from it, they work hard to make sure the idea works.

In today's Conceptual Age, asking for ideas from the workforce is the smart thing to do.

Think about your specific business for a minute. Each of your employees has their own unique view of the business, depending on what their job is.

They have a different view of the way things work than you do. They could tell you things about your business that you might not realize. They could probably think of ideas to help the business run better, safer, or with less waste.

When a person performs the same tasks (or observes others doing their duties) day after day, they're able to come up with ideas to improve processes, save money, or increase productivity.

Some of them bring ideas for improvement from places where they used to work. They might walk in and see a problem you've been struggling with for a long time and be able to fix it in less than a day.

Simply put, ideas are money. Make sure you're doing everything you can to capture them and put them to work in your business.

In reality, I don't know how any large corporation can afford *not* to have some sort of suggestion program.

Think about it. In the age where ideas and concepts are regularly leveraged to boost the bottom line, do you want a *few* minds focused on improving the business or **all of them**?

Factory Flow

Once you understand how negativity holds your business back, you'll start to see opportunity in places you'd never before thought to look.

For example, the time I spent in manufacturing taught me a very valuable lesson about the way energy flows through ANY workforce.

"Factory flow" is a common term used to describe the way materials flow through a manufacturing facility. Factories perform the best when raw goods flow in, move steadily through the process, and continue out the back door to the customer without interruption.

If a machine or operation causes a "bottleneck" or a restriction in the flow of parts, teams of experts are called upon to focus on the challenge until they figure out how to get the "value stream" moving again.

These teams are highly trained in advanced problem-solving techniques designed to help them quickly get to the root cause of the problem.

Bottlenecks can happen for a variety of reasons. Some common ones are: machine breakdowns, bad tooling from the supplier, bad production stock, material handling problems, quality issues, etc.

Trust me, the list of crazy things that can stop production in a manufacturing facility is endless - and sometimes unbelievable.

Once the problem is identified, the machine is fixed (or the situation is rectified), and production resumes. After a reasonable amount of time has passed, the bottleneck is reevaluated to make sure the solution was an effective one.

Because, if there's one thing that EVERYONE in manufacturing understands, it's that time is money.

But manufacturing isn't the only business where bottlenecks are costing the company money. There are 'bottlenecks' of various types in every business.

Negativity works the same way in your workforce as a broken machine on the factory floor. It limits your company's ability to flow, and it ultimately steals momentum and money.

Because they now realize that negativity is manageable, today's smart managers are taking a different look at their workforce to identify pockets of negativity and areas of opportunity.

They're focusing on the flow of their workforce.

When trouble spots are identified, specially trained experts are brought in to analyze these 'bottlenecks' and figure out effective solutions. These teams are trained in advanced communication techniques designed to help them understand complex situations from each individual's unique perspective.

The process to resolve critical issues can vary from situation to situation, but the most important factor is that the issues are dealt with in a positive, consistent manner.

By handling "bottlenecks" in this way, employees can be gently refocused on the expectation of professionalism as part of a high-performance team with a common goal.

It's important to remember that negativity is almost always opportunity in disguise.

Business Synergy

So, do you think I've gotten a little far from my original topic of Unsocial Media Management? I'll admit, I've strayed a bit from putting bullies in their place.

But if you remember correctly, I warned you in the Introduction that the main focus of this book is not about negative people.

"You see, the negativity that plagues social media isn't the primary focus of *Unsocial Media Management for Business.*"

My goal is to help you to prosper. Focusing on negative people won't help you do that.

Although it may seem like I've gone off track, everything I've done up to this point has been deliberate. Unsocial Media Management was just my "hook" to get your attention.

My underlying goal has always been to teach you a simple process to crank up the energy in your business. And I mean that quite literally. You'll learn to do it in the next chapter.

But before we can flip on the BIG MONEY switch, there's one more lesson you need to learn.

Actually, I'd call it more of a shift in perspective. You just learned in "Factory Flow" how energy flows through your workforce, and that pockets of negativity disrupt your value stream.

If you're up to speed on that, you're most of the way there. The next step?

Imagine your business as one integrated machine with energy that flows throughout, like the electrical system on a vehicle.

This encompasses everyone who is associated with or affected by your business. It starts with your suppliers, travels through your workforce, and radiates out into your customers, prospects, critics, and fans.

Call it your business heartbeat if you want to.

Do you remember when I told you that negativity anywhere in your business (value stream) is costing you money? The whole thing is really all about energy flow.

Think of the negativity that used to hold you back as being similar to an electrical "short" in your company's operating system. That's why I taught you to deal with negativity first. Repairing the "shorts" in a machine's electrical system is the first step any electrician would have to take to get it going again.

The second step was to build a solid foundation (business brand) to communicate from. By doing this, you're strengthening the structure of your electrical system and learning new ways (authentic examples) to reroute energy to benefit you.

The purpose of this chapter (and the last one) is to show you where to look for prosperity and to make sure you're not being held back by old ideas. It's also meant to cause you to take another look at your current business model to see if there are opportunities to replace old ideas and technology (update your circuits) with ones that are more up-to-date.

Don't hesitate to go back to Chapter Two and rebrand yourself as the expert if you have to. You'll be better off in the long run if you start off on the right foot.

Take the time to shape your business into a high-performance Conceptual Age machine. Build it right. Then roll up your sleeves and meet me back here.

Because once you've let go of the things that aren't serving your bottom line and made sure all systems are GO, it's time to crank your business up to FULL POWER.

Are you ready to energize your bottom line?

CHAPTER 7

Energize Your Bottom Line

You're ready.

You've learned to free yourself from the negative influences that have been holding you back from social media success.

You know why negative people do what they do.

You understand how (and why) to prepare yourself for harassment, negativity, and insults.

You recognize the true value of giving an authentic response when a negative person attacks.

You see how the harassment you'd previously avoided can be leveraged into an opportunity for a positive interaction.

You've taken a good look at everything your company does to make sure you're not wasting time or energy on outdated ideas and old ways of doing things.

And you see your business as a powerful machine with energy that flows throughout everything you do.

If you understand these lessons, you're ready to move on to the final step.

It's time to flip the switch that energizes the people who will add zeroes to your bottom line.

Charged Up

You know how it feels to be 'charged up' about something, right?

Think about the times when you've been inspired, motivated, or energized by some new thing you've encountered.

When you're excited about something, you want to learn everything there is to know about it. You enjoy and appreciate it, and see how others enjoy and appreciate it, too. Then you tell your friends about it, and the energy keeps flowing.

When your audience is charged up about your product, service, or company, they buy more products, utilize more services, click more links, share more information, and are more likely to protect your business as if it were their own.

Charged up people in your business and your customer base spread positive energy to those around them, and the effects ripple out from there.

One happy customer on a popular blog or review site can trigger thousands of sales.

One charged up person in your sales department can raise the energy, expectation, and performance of the whole team.

One tiny jolt of positive energy in the right area of your business can result in a big boost to your bottom line.

But how do you use social media to charge your audience up about your product, service, brand, or business?

It's simple.

Charging people up works the same as anything else that runs on electricity...

People Run on Electricity

Most of us don't fully realize it, but people run on electricity. Each of our heartbeats is a small electrical charge. Our brain waves are electrical currents. Every thought we have and every move we make is powered by electricity.

Even the way we *feel* is electrical.

But again - what does this have to do with marketing or creating a better attitude in your workforce?

Although people don't have power cords, they *can* be charged up.

It's a simple process. First, you get their attention, or "plug them in." Then you make them feel better, or "charge them up."

It's a new approach to online communication, and it works great when applied to social media marketing and influence.

Think about it. People run on electricity.

Stress, drama, and negativity run us down. The things we like and appreciate charge us up. You know it's true based on the way various influences make you feel.

Once you understand that you can literally generate more energy inside others by communicating intentionally, you'll interact in a more purposeful way.

90% Opportunity?

Have you ever heard the scientific theory that humans only use about 10% of their available brain power?

I didn't believe it when I first heard it, but I did like the idea of there being 90% opportunity for growth inside each of us.

When I investigated this claim, I found out that the 10% figure was an estimated average of available brain power used during the course of a day while a normal person is awake.

In a nutshell, human beings generate more power when focused on something exciting or interesting and less when performing boring (low-energy) tasks like watching television or doing repetitive work. The overall average was 10 percent.

They needed a study for this? It seems like common sense to me, but I suppose it raises an interesting question.

Could there be an actual *electrical* reason why we're able to quickly learn and remember everything there is to know about the things we're interested in (like a hobby) but can't remember any details about the things that don't interest us (like Algebra), even when we try our hardest?

And have you ever tried to learn something while you were sad, depressed, angry, or stressed? It's not easy at all.

When you think about it this way, doesn't it make sense that we generate *more* brainpower when we're excited or stimulated (positive) and *less* when we're uninterested, sad, or stressed (negative)?

For the record, I still don't believe we only use 10% of our available brain power, but it makes sense to me that we'd use more when we're stimulated and less when we're not interested.

And although I prefer to think that we **MUST** use at least *half a brain* to get through our day (I think I used almost 87% of mine one time), I'm **certain** that we haven't come anywhere close to unleashing our full potential yet.

Regardless of the actual percentage, you'd almost have to agree that there's a lot of opportunity for *some* people to use more of their brain.

The Emotional Scale

How are you feeling right now?

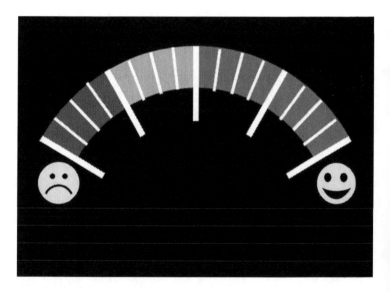

You might feel *excited* to learn the process of charging your audience up. You might feel *bored* because your employer is making you read this stupid book. Or you may feel *angry* that I'm talking about electricity in a book that's supposed to be about social media.

The way you're feeling right now (about any given subject) falls somewhere on an emotional scale that ranges from the lowest of lows (like hopelessness and despair) to the most energized feelings (like elation and inspiration).

When we're excited about a new hobby, interest, or passion, our energy is toward the top end of the emotional scale.

When we're stressed or bored, we're hanging out more toward the bottom.

It's pretty easy to understand.

Love, hate, happy, sad, angry, goofy, etc. They all fall somewhere on the emotional scale.

Think about how certain subjects make you feel. What do you like? What can't you stand? Who is your favorite musician or band? Are you a fan of reality shows?

We feel differently about various influences, topics, people, situations, memories, experiences, examples, and so on.

As we move through the course of our day, we experience a wide range of emotion on various subjects as we encounter different influences. You might feel happy when you think of your kids or your dog, but sad or angry when you think of money or politics.

It's the same for your target audience. Each topic they focus on presents an opportunity to connect with them on another emotional level. (Like plugging in a power cord.)

When you consider everything that goes on in people's lives, isn't it obvious that there are literally thousands of ways to meet someone where they're at on the emotional scale?

And although many of the subjects on social media are closer to the bottom than the top, it really doesn't matter if the discussion starts off positive or negative.

The only thing that matters is if you can move your audience *up* the emotional scale from where they're at.

To be effective at social media marketing and influence, connect with your audience where they're at and move them up the emotional scale (charge them up) to a better feeling place.

Meet Them Where They're at

The first step in charging anything up is to plug it in. People are no different.

As previously stated (for the purpose of charging your audience up), the way to 'plug them in' is to meet them where they're at on the emotional scale.

This is the marketing "hook" I told you about in Chapter Four.

In today's busy digital world, there are more advertisements than ever before in history. The hook has become even more important than it used to be.

To understand the hook in 'charged up' terms, it actually helps to think about a *bad* hook first. One way a hook can really miss the mark is by trying to communicate with someone on a completely different emotional level than they're on.

For example, if someone was feeling depressed and you were to walk past them whistling and laughing, you probably wouldn't be able to effectively communicate with them. (Some would say you weren't on the same vibrational level.)

Your taste in music is also a good way to think about being able to connect on an emotional level. You might love an artist or band that would quickly drive others from the room.

And how do you feel about people who talk too much in the early morning? I don't like it either. It's hard for me to communicate with someone whose lips are flapping 90 miles an hour at 6 am. I've actually told people to "come back after I've had a coffee and you've had a chance to calm down."

Anyhow...

Effective communication requires that you connect on an emotional level.

Take this book for example.

If I would have said, "Hey, I'm going to tell you how to use social media to get your audience to buy more of your products by plugging them in because people run on electricity and...", you never would have bought this book.

Instead, I developed the 'Unsocial Media Management' concept to meet you at your *"frustrated with social media"* emotional level, and it's proven to be a good hook for delivering my 'charged up' message.

Because that's what I really want. I want you to feel energized and prosperous.

One of the big economic advantages of the internet and social media is that you can connect and communicate with a greater number of people (or various specific groups) on a more personal level than ever before.

Connecting...

Some businesses prefer traditional marketing methods that turn the features of their product or service into benefits and communicate to their customer based on their needs.

When you think about it, most of those types of advertisements try to meet their audience on a lower emotional level as well. Their point of connection is the way their prospect feels when he or she needs what they have to offer.

If your business, cause, or brand doesn't require you to connect with your target audience through the benefits of your product or service, another opportunity to *plug them in* is to figure out where they're already focused and meet them there.

There are a lot of ways to do this. You can read through the posts and comments in related groups or check out your competitor's pages. Some businesses send out customer surveys with rewards or discounts for completing them.

If you want to take the guesswork out of what your audience likes, today's profiling and targeting tools are extremely powerful because of the way the internet collects marketing information. You can easily find all the resources you'll need by performing a simple "marketing and targeting tools" internet search.

Sometimes we choose to communicate on a topic based on a unique opinion, vision, or perspective that we've developed through something we experienced. Don't be afraid to try new things. Short, personal stories are social media gold.

Again, there are an endless number of ways to plug your audience in. The methods and topics that fit your business needs the best will depend on the type of organization you run, your business goals, and whether or not you have a knack for moving people up the emotional scale.

To help you to better understand the idea of meeting a target audience on an emotional level, I've included the following six examples:

1. Real estate prospects who are feeling down because of the drab winter weather.
2. A power washing audience that witnessed an online attack on your business.
3. A group of out of work (or underemployed) skilled trades who are open to the idea of a new career path or side business.
4. A workforce that is angry about the second round of budget cuts.
5. Potential affiliates who are tired of seeing negativity on social media.
6. Customers who were sent the wrong product by mistake.

Again, these are simply examples of audiences and their emotional levels on specific topics. In the next couple of sections, I'll go deeper into these same examples so you can learn how to meet them where they're at and move them up the emotional scale.

Charge Them Up

After you understand where your target audience is at on the emotional scale, it's time to charge them up.

By charging them up, I mean to share a message or idea that meets them where they're at and causes them to feel better in some way.

To understand it more clearly, check out the following example (1 of 6 from above):

If you're a real estate agent looking to use social media to drum up some sales on a slow winter day, you might post something like the following on your Facebook Page:

"If you're tired of that same old view outside your window, I can help you upgrade to one that gives you a warmer, happier feeling when you look outside. I'm impressed with some of the beautiful properties that have recently come available on the market, and I think you will be too."

You could even add a picture of a drab wintery day looking out the window at a shambles of a property and another overlooking a beautiful yard in the summertime.

Remember, meet them where they're at.
As I write this, it's mid-March and snowing in Michigan. People are complaining about it all over social media. They're ready for winter to be over. The view outside their window is not pleasing to them, and neither is the temperature.

Using the principles outlined in this chapter, you can use both to your advantage. Meet them where they're at...

Then charge them up.

As a realtor, you can't change the weather, but you *do* provide the service of changing the view outside their window. Help them to "see" it from where they're at, then help them to "feel" something better.

While I'm not a fan of fear-based marketing, there's nothing wrong with using the dismal picture that Mother Nature has painted outside their window to connect with them on the emotional level they're on that day.

Drop in keywords (tired, same old view) to connect with the way they feel or to match the situation they're in. Then move them up the emotional scale with better-feeling words (warmer, happier, upgrade).

Connect them with a better feeling, then sell them a home with a better view.

On Monday when you post your "deal of the week," they might ask about the view out the window, which you're able to provide on that same thread easily, along with a few questions to pre-qualify them. Others will be curious about the view as well, and BOOM! That house is sold.

In reality, this is the way a lot of marketing already works. Looking at it from an electrical perspective is just another way to think about the marketing process.

If you're interested in finding out more about using this "Charged Up" marketing concept, pick up your free copy of *Charged Up Marketing* (http://www.unsocialmedia management.com/bonus) if you haven't already.

Five Charged Up Examples

As promised, here are the other examples that identify the person communicating, their audience, the emotional level they're on, and ideas for charging them up.

1. The Power Wash Challenge

A different power washing friend of mine posted before and after pictures of a fleet truck he'd washed to his Facebook business page.

One guy repeatedly called him a liar and a fraud on that post. This went on for days. When things got too far out of control, he panicked and deleted the post and the pictures.

The attacker immediately went nuts on his page and also started posting in different groups and forums saying my friend had been caught in a lie and that he'd verified it by taking the fraudulent pictures down. The naysayer said it wasn't the same truck because the serial number had been different in the picture (it wasn't) and there was NO WAY the truck could have been the same from as dirty as it had begun.

Upon watching this situation unfold, I advised my friend to publicly and respectfully invite the disbeliever to the next washing of that **same truck** and *offer to pay him for his time and travel expenses,* which he immediately did.

When the attacker declined (as we both knew he would), I instructed my friend to follow up with a 30-second time-lapse video of the truck being washed that included a personalized message simply thanking the viewer for their time.

He went back and found all the old posts calling him a fraud and dropped that video link on every one. The video was viewed a LOT of times because of the controversy leading up to it.

We never could have gotten that many views from an ordinary truck washing video. As a result, his social media following **doubled** in just a few weeks (after a whole year of slow growth) and he picked up enough accounts to fill his schedule.

In this example, the hook was obviously the drama of repeatedly being called a liar. The "charging them up" came when the business owner did everything in his power to act respectful and was successful in proving without a doubt that he was not a fraud.

2. A Conceptual Age Opportunity for Skilled Trades

In today's economy, it's not uncommon to hear about skilled tradespeople who can't find steady work.

Every economic sector expands and contracts, and the trades have taken a huge hit lately. From working in both career sectors, it's obvious to me that there's currently more opportunity in copywriting and web design than in skilled trades.

But how do you go from being a skilled tradesman to a website designer? Easy. You buy a course.

Web design is a natural fit for people who understand construction and architecture.

Believe it or not, the structure of a website is similar to the structure of a building. Websites have different 'floors' and 'rooms' that are designed to flow into one another, just like any building.

I've known several craftsmen who made this career transition and quickly became very good at designing websites because of their technical ability.

To market a web design program to them, meet them where they're at (jobs hard to come by, have to drive, economic picture dismal) and charge them up (building skills will come in handy, growing sector of the economy, can work from home instead of driving to another state, and etc.) you can easily sell a $500 web copywriting course.

3. The Second Round of Cutbacks

Pretend you're a Corporate Manager who was just informed that you have to notify your workforce about YET ANOTHER round of budget cuts that nobody saw coming.

How do you keep your employees motivated when the going gets tough?

If it were my job, I'd come right out and say I regret the company's decision to implement these measures and that I wish there could have been some other decision. I'd also let them know I understand the impact these specific changes will have on their lives. I'd express my hope that the company's plan is effective in returning the business to profitability so those losses can be restored. After that, I'd encourage these valued employees to remember the gains that the workforce and company have made through the decades and remind them that the economy runs in cycles.

(I'm not asking you to sugarcoat the truth or to mislead anyone in any way. My point is that you will be a more powerful influencer by mixing in posts and comments that charge your audience up.)

To close, I'd thank them for the hard work they do, deliver whatever other messages need to be delivered, appreciate them for their continued professionalism, and sign my letter "Respectfully."

In this case, the hook is already there for you. The second round of budget cuts is where people start wondering if the company is ok or if they should jump ship. Now is the time for you to lead with a powerful message that preserves your experienced workforce as you negotiate the economic challenges in front of you.

The way to charge them up, in this case, is with a vision of better times to come. Make sure to stop short of seeming disillusioned, disconnected, or "puppy dogs and rainbows" instead of genuine.

[Note: They'll respond better if you've taken the time to establish a personalized (two-way) line of communication beforehand.]

4. How to Profit from Online Negativity

If you like the idea of making money by helping others overcome drama and negativity on social media, I can tell you how in three easy steps. (This example is real, by the way.)

Click here http://www.wp-amazon-plugin.com/register-amazon-affiliate-product-advertising-api/ to become an Amazon affiliate, share your affiliate link when you see examples of people who want better social media, and collect money automatically in your PayPal account when people buy my book through your link.

(In this case, *you* are my target audience, your emotional level is that you want better social media and more money, and my idea for charging you up is the fact that you can make an easy profit by helping others resolve their social media issues.)

5. A Customer Service Representative after Your Company Made a Mass Mistake

Pretend your company was supposed to send out 725 red widgets but your order fulfillment center accidentally sent all 725 customers each a purple doohickey by mistake.

Now it's your job to send out the email that explains the whole mess, and oh yeah...the CEO wants as many of those darned doohickeys back as possible.

If this was me, I'd start this email out by apologizing for the crazy mistake. Then I'd poke a little fun at the shipping people who can't tell a purple doohickey from a red widget.

To make a better connection with these widget lovers, I might share some reasons why people love red widgets so much. I'd make sure to appreciate them for doing business with my company and allowing us to be their widget supplier.

Then I'd assure these **valued customers** that their correct order is in the mail as we speak, accompanied by a return box to save that worthless purple doohickey from taking up space in a landfill. I might even include a discount offer for the first ten to come back.

Just because your company made a mistake doesn't mean you can't still find ways to charge your audience up. You just have to look for them.

Note: Just like you can't establish a connection from a mismatched emotional level, you also can't move people too far up the emotional scale at once. For example, you can't move them from despair to happiness or from anger into excitement. It's too far of a stretch. They won't be able to make the jump. Once you've come to understand where they're at emotionally on any given topic, simply aim to help them to feel better in some way. That's all.

Charging people up takes practice, finesse, and forethought. It's very similar to managing unsocial media. Both have the potential to attract negative feedback.

Some people feel threatened by powerful communicators. Even though you're just trying to charge people up, sooner or later some Negative Nancy will accuse you of being a fraud.

Still, that's okay. We know what to do with drama. In fact, it's easier for me to charge an audience up from a negative situation than it is to try to get their attention through regular marketing.

But it's my job to say that. I'm the Unsocial Media Management guy. It's what I do.

Unsocial Media Management IS Charged Up Marketing

Have you come to understand that this "Charged Up" concept is actually the very basis of Unsocial Media Management?

It's all about electricity.

You're meeting your audience in a lower place on the emotional scale (thanks to your attacker), then you're immediately moving them up by giving an authentic response.

Now, isn't it obvious that it's really not your attacker who matters? You're communicating with your target market, not just some jerk who wants to start trouble. (I didn't really mean that.) :)

Think about the Seven Authentic Examples from Chapter Three:

1. Appreciate their passion for the subject.
2. Respect their opinion and perspective.
3. Edify them for their strengths.
4. Find common ground.
5. Be openly compassionate.
6. Be willing to give a "pass."
7. Ask for questions/solutions.

Can you see how each of these responses is designed to move your audience (and your attacker) up the emotional scale?

If you consciously set out with the goal of charging people up, you'll be far less likely to fall into the traps of those who'd love to see you fail.

Do you understand that it's almost easier to leverage negative situations to charge your audience up because you're meeting them at a lower place on the emotional scale with more room to move them up?

And isn't it obvious how important it is to free yourself from negative situations before you can unleash the true power of social media for your business?

The Power of Communication

"The pen is mightier than the sword" - **Edward Bulwer-Lytton**, Novelist and Playwright, 1839.

Whether you understand the power of communication in electrical terms or not, I'm certain you realize that effective communication is indeed very powerful.

The above quote was written 178 years ago when *pens* were cutting-edge communication technology.

The author knew back then that one powerful communicator could potentially summon 10,000 people with swords using only pen and paper. (For the record, 10,000 wins against 1 EVERY time.)

So if the pen is mightier than the sword, just how powerful is today's social media, where the device you hold in your hand has the potential to communicate with every other device connected to the world wide web around the globe?

I can't even begin to put that amount of power into words. To me, it's powerful beyond measure.

But let's be honest, you've known all along that social media was powerful. In fact, the reason some of you bought this book in the first place was because you were worried about those ten thousand swords coming after *you* someday.

But thankfully, that's all behind you now.

You've learned to manage online negativity and turn it into better things. You understand how to communicate effectively.

You know how to leverage the true power of social media, which is to create a place where people feel good when they come into contact with your business.

Because people will always remember the way you made them feel.

That's the true power of social media.

If your business, brand, or logo makes them feel better when they see it, they'll think of you as 'their go-to guy.'

And that's about the best you can do.

So that's it. Plug them in. Charge them up. Make them feel better. Make them feel empowered.

If you're successful in doing that, they'll buy more products, utilize more services, click more links, share more information, and be more likely to protect your business as if it were their own.

Good luck!

Your Feedback is Greatly Appreciated!

Please leave an honest review by visiting www.amazon.com

Thanks again for reading my book. I really appreciate your feedback, and I LOVE hearing what you have to say.

If something in my book has inspired, motivated, or energized you in some way, I'd greatly appreciate it if you would take the time to leave a review.

Likewise, if you think that some (or all) of what I've said here is inaccurate or complete and utter nonsense, I encourage you to leave a review.

Because I want to hear what you have to say. It helps me to grow and improve.

This book is full of my unique ideas and opinions, and I've been wrong before. If you're successful in proving me wrong, I'll be the first to admit it and I will amend my book to match the facts.

If you just want to be a pain in the butt and harass me, you'll give me something to write about in my next book. As I state in one of my promotions, this may be the only book on the market that invites negative reviews.

For the record, most of the people who write bad reviews never read the entire book. Those people are easy to flush out and make an example of.

But since you've read this far, I trust you've gotten some value from what I've written. If so, I'd be honored if you would reach out in some way to share your experiences and perspectives. Because my intent is to help you to grow and prosper.

I appreciate you, and I wish you all the best.

About the Author

Brandy Booth is an author, copywriter, skilled tradesman, mediator, facilitator, positive influencer, and proponent of change.

From 2002-2011, he served the membership of the United Auto Workers as committeeman, contract negotiator, skilled trades delegate, and Sergeant at Arms. In that capacity, he received training in collective bargaining, conflict resolution through mediation, advanced communication techniques, and several other programs focused on resolving issues between employees, managers, contractors, and people in general.

During that time, he also became a facilitator of Lou Tice's *Pacific Institute*, a corporate training program designed to empower employees to recognize and adapt to the tough changes facing the auto industry during bankruptcy reorganization and restructuring.

After that, his focus turned to copywriting and marketing with a special interest in social media. Brandy has helped several business owners and managers find ways to streamline and improve their businesses through advancements in technology and communication.

His experience in helping others to recognize and overcome negativity motivated him to launch the *Unsocial Media Management* book series in 2017.

Brandy resides in Michigan with his wife and four children. In his spare time, he enjoys spending time with his family, fishing, riding his motorcycle, playing guitar, and helping others to focus on the things in life they appreciate.

Where to Next?

Are you excited by what you've just learned and wondering how to apply these concepts to your personal social media accounts?

The next book in the series, *Unsocial Media Management for Personal Use: Your 'How-to' Guide for Reducing Drama, Creating a Positive News Feed, and Being a Powerful Influencer*, is due out in the fall of 2017.

That book focuses on the personal aspects of social media, like managing your news feed for a more positive experience and dealing with those pesky negative people who always seem to come out of the woodwork when you least expect them to.

Although the books are similar (after all, negativity **is** negativity), the personal book is designed specifically for day-to-day personal social media users who want to communicate with friends and family or talk in groups without the fear of being attacked.

It makes a great gift for people who want a better social media experience without the stress, drama, and negativity that sometimes blindsides us as we're going about our day.

You can learn more about how to get your hands on a copy of this book at www.unsocialmediamanagement.com.

And if you haven't yet picked up your free PDF copy of Charged Up Marketing, you can do so http://www.unsocialmediamanagement.com/bonus.

Affiliate / Coauthoring Opportunity

If you'd like to learn a simple process to make a profit by sharing the lessons in this book with others who could use it, click http://www.unsocialmediamanagement.com/affiliate/.

And if you're a well-known expert in your field who would like to discuss coauthoring an Unsocial Media Management book for your target market, feel free to email me at brandy@unsocialmediamanagement.com.

Made in the USA
Middletown, DE
16 August 2017